Third Time at Bat

A MEMOIR OF MARRIAGES

LEIGH DAVIS

This book is a work of nonfiction. Some names and identifying details of people described in this book have been altered to protect their privacy.

Copyright © 2021 by Leigh Davis

All rights reserved. This book may not be reproduced or stored in whole or in part by any means without the written permission of the author except for brief quotations for the purpose of review.

ISBN: 978-1-954614-34-5

Davis. Leigh.
Third Time at Bat

Edited by: Beth Crosby, Karli Jackson, and Monika Dziamka

Published by Warren Publishing
Charlotte, NC
www.warrenpublishing.net
Printed in the United States

"NEVER LET THE FEAR OF STRIKING OUT KEEP YOU FROM PLAYING THE GAME."

—BABE RUTH

*This book is dedicated to women who need
to gather their inner strength to lift themselves up,
to fly away from abusive relationships,
and to find joy in their own soaring free spirits.*

CHAPTER ONE

Pre-game Warm-Up

In 1954, when my mom and dad knew parenthood was nearing, they realized their dream of moving from the bustling city of Philadelphia to a sleepy country village. I grew up in Warrington, which consisted of a few middle-class developments surrounded by acres of farmland and forests. Nearby dairy farms provided milk delivered to our doorstep in glass bottles by Floyd The Milkman. The nearby fields and forests afforded hunters like my dad an abundant supply of deer, pheasant, rabbit, and squirrel. The tarred, two-lane country roads were lightly traveled, ideal for bike-riding teenagers.

It was a short bike ride from my home to my best friend Sharon's home, a brick rancher on a corner lot. We had just celebrated our fifteenth birthdays, eighteen days apart, in the spring of 1970. I hastily leaned my blue Schwinn bike against the concrete wall of the covered porch connecting her garage to the kitchen and called through the screen door.

"Sharon, are you home? I sure need to talk!"

Her twin brother came to the door. "She's in her room. Go on back."

"Teach Your Children" by Crosby, Stills, Nash, and Young played throughout the house. The lyrics spoke to me on that day, for the first of many times to come.

I found her sprawled across her bed doing homework. "Sharon! My parents told me not only to get a job, but that my toiletries, accessories, and make-up are my responsibility from now on!" I vented, eyes narrowed, to the closest person I had to a sister. What felt like punishment then was my first life lesson in molding a strong work ethic.

"Join the club. The same edict was given to me," she replied. But then she offered, "Let's go job-hunting together." Maybe she wasn't a blood sister, but this shared pain was balm to my only-child status.

Shortly thereafter we crossed the field between my backyard and the town's only strip mall. Our first stop was Christiansen's Gift Shop. The owner, Peg Christiansen, greeted our job request with an amused smile and proceeded to acknowledge that she was aware of my identity.

"Sorry, there are no positions open right now. You are both welcome to apply. And how are your parents doing, Leigh?"

My parents attended the same church as this large-boned, red-headed, freckled, Irish lady with a hearty laugh and a contagious smile. One of my earliest memories was her envious gaze at my mother, who held me in her arms as a toddler. She always complimented me in some way.

"She doesn't have any children. She has a nice gift shop instead," Mom told me early on.

Mrs. Christiansen's warm, approving smile drew me to her, even as a small child in church. Decades later I would sob at her funeral.

Sharon and I walked home across the field. I stopped, turned to look at the back of the store, and said, "Of course there are no openings. That's the premiere job of jobs for teenagers in this town. Imagine getting paid to sell such beautiful gifts and making fancy bows to adorn them all!"

"At least you have an in because of your parents," Sharon scoffed. "But I bet she doesn't know how cheap they are."

The summer before, my parents had allowed Sharon to come along on vacation with us. In a rented Winnebago we traveled the East Coast up to Maine. But they made it conditional: "She has to bring her own spending money."

Our most exciting adventure was getting lost in the dunes of Cape Cod. Mom and Dad never knew. We probably gave them time for intimacy during our three-hour absence. Ever affectionate with one another, their playful kisses and flirtatious innuendo were plentiful, and their shared sense of humor was infectious. I knew I wanted this kind of relationship someday.

Bodily functions were hard to hide in close quarters on this trip; thus, Dad christened us "little turd" and "little fart." Sharon giggled at this since her father was too stern to kid about such things and would never be seen cuddling her mom on the sofa as my parents often did.

My friendship with Sharon had been years in the making. She had soothed me on our first day of kindergarten. I had decided I didn't like kindergarten because the teacher was brand new to the school, so I bolted out the door and ran straight home. My mother promptly returned me to class. A blonde girl with cat-like eyes, wearing a pink-flowered headband, came to my side.

"Don't cry, little girl," I remember her saying. "I will play with you today. My name is Sharon. What's yours?"

We became life-long friends, our idyllic childhoods in Warrington fostering our initial bond. Because an only child is often a lonely one, our formative and genuine friendship grew.

We did get hired together for our first jobs that summer—as telemarketers. We sat at a table going through phone books, marking down phone book pages, dialing on black rotary phones, selling educational courses to veterans, and earning a whole dollar an hour. Our work break treat was a freshly baked vanilla creme donut at nearby Kirshner's bakery for a mere dime.

We soon found jobs that let us buy a lot more donuts with our wages—as waitresses. Sharon went north to Friendly's, and I headed south to a breakfast café run by two elderly sisters. I was young and naïve and attracted way too many males to please the hardened career waitresses, but I worked there briefly until that fateful call at last came in from Mrs. Christiansen to become one of her gift shop girls.

My pay rate increased to $1.25 per hour through my high school years and holiday seasons in college. My job was to help customers find their perfect gift, then wrap it in the back room using one of the huge rolls of elegant wrapping paper hung horizontally on metal rods. Organza butterflies or sprigs of delicate flowers sprang from the centers of the fluffy bows we hand-cranked out. I quickly grew to admire the proprietors, Mr. and Mrs. C, as the salesgirls addressed them.

Mrs. C told me on a slow night before closing that her current husband was not her first. This was certainly a shocker, as I had never contemplated her life without her current husband. She had divorced a doctor who broke her heart after returning from the war in love with another nurse. Mrs. C had been a supervising nurse, as was her only sister, Jean. Her current husband had been a merchant marine and began bringing her exotic artifacts from his travels after their marriage. When it was clear they would not have their own children and an adoption fell through, they decided to go into business selling fine gifts. Mrs. C became the kind mother she always wanted to be—to her store girls. She was a stern businesswoman with a caring heart, a perfect second mom to me, gentle in her criticism but tough when she needed to be. Her nickname was Eagle Eyes, as *nothing* got past her. She could turn away a salesman of low-quality merchandise with just one look when he came through the huge glass entrance doors.

She gave me hell once after my visit to Villanova, a Catholic University about an hour from home. A boy there named Boston had become my pen pal. After a few months of correspondence, Boston invited me to visit him one weekend. My friend Cherie said she knew the way there. Her mom actually allowed Cherie to borrow the family car. The boys were cute and friendly enough when we arrived at their dorm. They pulled out a bottle of deep purple potion from under a bed.

"Do you like blackberry brandy?" Boston asked like an eager, panting puppy.

"Don't know. Never tried it," I said.

Boston retrieved foam cups from his closet. The smell of berries and syrup filled my nostrils. Yum. He filled the cup to the brim, and my first whole cup of alcohol went down smoothly. Cherie said I passed out, and later I learned that they hurriedly hid me in the communal shower while the monsignor made his rounds. My only memory of that night was Cherie getting my house key out of my purse on my parents' doorstep at midnight. That is precisely when I sobered up. My adrenaline rushed, my pulse quickened, and my muscles tensed as my thoughts raced to make sense of the plan she was describing to me.

"Now I'm leaving you. Once you're inside, quietly crawl up the steps and into your bed."

I remember my mother stirring from her sleep. Thankfully she did not arise from her bed.

She yelled, "Glad you're home. Don't forget Mrs. C wants you to open the store with her at nine sharp."

Oh crap!

The next morning, Mrs. C. took one look at me when I entered the gift shop, then sniffed my face.

"You are in-corr-ig-ible…. Go home and look it up. Now."

My knees weakened; my face tingled as it reddened.

At home, I learned that the word means "cannot be reformed due to bad habits." *Note to self: Do not go to work hungover.* Luckily, my second mom forgave me. I am not sure my real mom ever knew, as I followed Cherie's instructions to a tee. My first drinking-girlfriend was from a teetotaling Baptist family, and she was my savior that night!

***

I attended Tamanend Junior High School, named after a long-departed Indian chief. When I was promoted into the school, something called "tracking" existed in the educational system. My placement in class 7-1 meant that in all academic studies, I was among the two dozen who had scored highest on their IQ tests. In effect, we were in a stellar class of intellectually gifted students who challenged one another and, often, the teacher. Competition was keen. God forbid if class 7-2 outdid us—ever. Conversely, those in class 7-9 were labeled intellectually challenged. Sadly, they were immediately ostracized by other students, and their teachers dumbed down their lesson plans.

In 7-1, most everyone in my class played a musical instrument. Band was the cool place to be. My parents bought me a used saxophone, and I began taking one-on-one lessons with our charismatic band teacher. Though my friendship continued with Sharon in 7-3, my new friend was Nancy in 7-1 who played the clarinet. She had long, straight blonde hair that swung down her small frame. She inspired me to keep up with her higher grades. Make-up, under-wire bras, and the Bee Gees became our new best friends. Suddenly, my body was voluptuous, and peers grew kinder, it seemed. Being slightly Rubenesque would thereafter be my asset, more than my downfall. My body would sway boyfriends to fall fast and hard, until they hit the brick wall of my virginity. This newfound power increased my self-worth until the first time I was dumped, whereupon it became a foundation of mistrust and hormonal confusion.

About this time, I was confirmed in my church, suffering through boring classes taught by a minister who was equally boring at the pulpit. His parishioners yawned with blank stares during his sermons. When taking my First Communion, I vowed to be a good girl. This meant remaining a virgin through high school, not becoming a pothead or an alcoholic, and never, ever riding on motorcycles.

My early relationship with faith and religion was simply an exercise in parental expectation. With an idyllic childhood, my life had not thrown any dangerous curveballs my way. There was little talk in our formal Lutheran church about a personal relationship with Christ. I couldn't desire a spiritual relationship that I didn't know was possible.

By ninth grade, I was tooting well enough on the saxophone to take second chair in my section. My long, light brown straight hair hung to the middle of my back, and my breasts had developed to more than my mother's B cup. My first date was with Jim, a trumpet player, to an event at his synagogue. He gave me my first kiss as his mother drove us back to Warrington. After Jim bragged about that kiss to the trombone section, Joe asked me out. He had already been flirting with me in Mr. Schreiner's literature class, where we were enthralled by our required classics: *The Pearl*, *David Copperfield*, *Siddhartha*, *Les Miserables*, and *Catcher in the Rye*. Mr. Schreiner was a fabulous teacher who wooed us with great books in an effort to hook us. If only Joe could have stimulated me intellectually, too, but he was in the pothead clique.

After only a few times getting high, I realized that pot made me feel stupid, lazy, and paranoid. Pot certainly did not make me want to go "all the way," as Joe had hoped. So, when we went on our band trip to Atlantic City, I traded the trombonist for a drummer, Schuyler. But when Schuyler wanted more than my kisses the time we snuck behind the low-rate motel, he dumped me for the bespectacled clarinetist, Judy, who gave him all he lusted for. Such were the short-lived band romances of junior high, then of monumental importance to naïve, overly-emotional teenage girls just like me.

Gymnastics felt natural to me in junior high gym class. Ms. Mullins gave me A's on floor and balance beam routines, which came easily. She told me I was the best in the school on the uneven parallel bars. That designation earned me the coveted final routine in the gym show.

I even made up my own dismount with a backward flip pushed off of the top bar. The yearbook included my photo with the caption, "She demonstrates how easy it is to fly." To continue with gymnastic lessons would only be a dream, though, as my parents saw absolutely no value in doing so. My dad was too busy soldiering and studying to further his daughter's only athletic ability.

***

High school began with a related activity, cheerleading. Sharon and I were determined to make the junior varsity squad, and we did. With our long, straight hair; short, plaid, black-and-gold skirts; and pom-poms, we were branded the "Rah-Rahs." The whole concept of chasing a ball over a line was inane to me. If it were a lobster or a diamond, it might make sense, but a ball? I did not know an offense cheer from a defense one but quickly learned when *not* to initiate "Push 'em back!" In all honesty, cheerleading was just a means to get dates. So what if we won or lost? I simply was not raised to care about who won in athletic contests!

Accelerated math and science classes were required for 10-1. Our teachers told us we needed to play Cold War catch-up with those meddling Russians. These were classes I had zero interest in. Trigonometry, physics, and advanced statistics were simply frightening, so I developed coping skills, like convincing the brainy class nerd to be my lab partner. In critical times like these, male manipulation was a valuable tool in helping me to raise my grades.

Tragedy struck in eleventh grade. Sharon made varsity cheerleading, leaving me in the dirt emotionally when I did not make the squad. I was co-captaining the JV squad with Jan, and she had something I longed for: Patrick, in 11-1 with me and the star quarterback. In German class, *I* was Pat's brainy nerd. This big Romeo with wandering hands was tall and muscular with Jagger's swagger. He was Roman Catholic, and that was a dating taboo. Because Jan had dibs on him and Dad forbid me to date Patrick, we flirted constantly and secretly went for rides, during which occurred lingering touches, quickened breaths, and a fluttering in our chests. My playing with fire never sparked because he would not break up with Jan, though I warned him about what my dad had said, that Italian gals get chunky with age. (Jan was unrecognizable at our last reunion; Dad had been correct!)

A cheerleader's motto was "Tease but don't please." By my senior year, I had many dates, yet no one would go steady with me because I would not put out. Once those hormonal beasts learned their particular charms and hollow lines had no effect on this busty girl, they moved on to another who would give them their release. Meanwhile, Sharon, Nancy, and Cherie had steadies. They all gave up what my mother had sworn was the most holy and sacred state a woman could possess. I channeled my frustration into my studies, acing all those advanced classes, placing as a national merit scholarship finalist, and ranking in the top tenth of my class. But I yearned to go steady with a guy, preferably one who would croon in angst to me like Marvin Gaye. Whenever a "going steady ring" would appear on a friend's finger, envy overtook me.

Then Sharon suffered the direst of consequences from going steady. She got pregnant.

She could not confide in her parents. Her dad, an elder in his church, told all three of his daughters they would be kicked out of his home pronto if they got pregnant, thereby disgracing the family with their obvious, growing sin. We knew this was no idle threat of his. She had saved a lot of money from her tips as a waitress.

"Would you please go with me to the clinic?" she pleaded to me one day. "My boyfriend can't handle going, and I would rather have you. Just come and hold my hand. You are my best friend."

Her mom thought we were going shopping at the mall. My next memory of that day was sitting in a cramped room with what looked like a blue vacuum cleaner. The smell of sterile antiseptic enveloped us. Sharon's face contorted in cramping pain during the abortion, and afterward, she looked ashen, drained of strength. She needed to have a good cry, but she insisted on driving, despite my objection.

"No, it's my mom's car, and I promised her no one else would drive it."

She really was a good girl and a dear friend. Maybe this "steady" thing was overrated.

Suddenly I recalled a memory from third grade. Sharon had come to school crying and confided to me that a man had pulled his car over and exposed himself to her. When I later told my mother, she said, "Well you must know, Sharon is a very pretty little girl, and you will never be as pretty as her."

I had felt broken inside. Time stopped. My thoughts spun. Was Mom glad I wasn't pretty? As a result, her daughter's prayer became, "Dear Jesus, make me pretty." Would my prayer be granted?

Maybe I hadn't been pretty enough to be a cheerleader in my senior year. The coach cut me at varsity auditions. Sharon made it and cheered until she gave up the hallowed position when she was voted in as our student counsel vice president. I admired her choice of brains over glamour. Furthermore, Sharon gave up cheerleading when it was an exciting time to be backing our undefeated football team. The team was coached by a Pennsylvania football legend, Mike Pettine, otherwise known as my history teacher. The games at our school wowed the fans.

In my senior year I finally landed a steady boyfriend, one who'd been in my kindergarten class.

A decade earlier, my most favorite teacher, Mrs. Esch, gave a pivotal lift to my self-esteem by casting me as Wendy in *Peter Pan*. Onstage, I felt euphoric.

"Tender Shepherd" was my first on-stage solo in a leading role. I first sang to Peter Pan: "Tender shepherd, let me help you count your sheep. One in the meadow, two in the garden, three in the nursery fast asleep." One day I would sing this lullaby to each of my babies before their bedtime.

Adorable Bobby, a shy neighbor, who lived around the bend and was one of my playmates as a toddler, played Peter. Sharon had also been cast…as a boy with a small solo.

I had previously played the Wicked Witch in *Snow White and the Seven Health Foods*, a kindergarten spin-off skit, but this was far more prestigious. Theater intrigued me. From that day forward I auditioned for every school play. Mrs. Esch had planted a seed. Wendy was a character longing to leave home with a beau who flew her to faraway adventures in exotic lands. What a fabulous life that would be!

The boy who was cast as Peter Pan grew into a tall, dark, and shy swim team member. From our first date, Bobby and I knew what we had in common. We liked to kiss passionately in the back seat of his dad's car with a cold bottle of cheap wine. We took in movies at the local cinema where we chose between *two* movies, went on the traveling carnival rides, or loitered with other teens at Burger King. We got caught necking at Stover's Park, so we found an alternative spot to park on Turkey Trot Road between two farmers' fields. Eventually, Bobby convinced me to smoke pot, thinking it would lead to the loss of my virginity. To his chagrin, it did not break me, literally. It made me cough and feel paranoid that we would be caught.

***

My parents permitted me to go on a summer vacation with Bobby and his older brother and sister. Before making the decision, Dad insisted on grilling Bobby's sister in our kitchen.

"Promise me they will be well-chaperoned with no funny business going on."

"Oh, yes, sir. I will read the Riot Act to both of them—especially to my little brother."

What Dad didn't know is Bobby had recently begged me to go all the way on prom night. I had declined.

Much to Bobby's delight, though, we were off to a secluded cove beach in rural South Carolina.

Two of his older brother's friends came along, watching me in wonderment as we clammed in the shallows. A strong wave jostled my breast out of my bikini top, as though collectively willed. Bobby surely had never felt so lucky. My already-sunburned face blushed behind my long, wind-blown hair.

Under a perfect, starry, summer Carolina sky, we slinked off to an isolated beach. I grabbed a towel, Bobby grabbed a condom unbeknownst to me, and there "it" happened. What surprised me was how quick and un-thrilling "it" was.

Clearly, the act scared Bobby out of his wits. The next day he avoided my gaze and nervously stuttered, "Because you are going to move away to college, it only makes sense for us to b-b-break up." Funny, he had not mentioned this idea before going to the beach the night before.

My sobbing ensued from that moment until his big sister dropped me at my front door with relief. The number one hit that week was Diana Ross singing, "Touch Me in the Morning," and every time it played on the car radio, I started blubbering. Hadn't I learned by now not to trust boys…or my mother? She met me at the door, took one look at my tear-stained, puffy face, and said, "You didn't give *it* away, did you?"

My inner actress declared, "*No way!*"

And with that settled, my mother handed me a newspaper.

"Think of those worse off than yourself for a change, like Mr. and Mrs. C. He's been in a horrible accident. He might not live."

She said this as she left me in the hall, sinking to the floor. Weakened from crying all day, it now felt as though I had been sucker-punched. Sensing my sadness, my loving, loyal mutt, Boots, comforted me, curling up in my arms that night.

The article told of a collision between a semi and Mr. C's white work van. His beloved boxer, who had been in the car with him, was euthanized at the scene. Mr. C was thrown many yards, landing on concrete. He clung to life in ICU.

When I went into work, the other sales girls told me more horrifying details. His head was swollen to double its normal size. Doctors could not say if he would ever walk or talk or even survive. All that Mrs. C prayed for was that God not take him from her. When I finally saw her, she clung to me, asking for prayers. Bobby breaking up with me took a back seat to seeing a beloved role model in such a despondent state of mind, her eyes reddened and her chin trembling.

I wouldn't be around for Mr. C's recovery that fall. I would attend a small liberal arts university in New Jersey almost two hours from home, double-majoring in psychology and theater. Broadway was just a short train ride away. Sharon chose to go to Brazil as an exchange student; Nancy went to the University of Pittsburgh; and Bobby attended the local agricultural college.

News eventually came from home that Mr. C had miraculously recovered, though he had changed from a gruff, masculine man to a whiny, effeminate religious fanatic. He claimed to have spoken with Jesus Christ Himself, who he said had given him a choice to go to Heaven with Him or to return to his wife. He chose the latter, giving his wife hell with frequent, unpredictable angry outbursts for the rest of her born days.

***

One night during the summer before college, while I was still home, my father answered the phone. He hung up, dropped his head, and cried like a baby. He had bad news: His father and namesake was dying from lung cancer.

Pop Norman was the first of my grandparents to die. My paternal grandparents lived in a brick row house with a windowless basement filled with shelf upon shelf of metal plumbing fixtures. Off of a small kitchen porch, Nana Meg and I used to throw scraps of white bread after our breakfast of poached eggs and toast. Hungry birds flocked daily to her backyard patch of grass out of habit.

Pop Norman was a loving and sweet-natured man most of the time. This was tested under two circumstances: if a broadcast of his beloved Phillies game was interrupted (green glass bottles of soda pop were presented to me as a quieting bribe), and when a novice in Pinochle misplayed a card. Then his stern glare followed.

Nana Meg was Pop's spunky, petite wife. She immigrated from Donegal, Ireland, as a young girl with her parents and six older siblings.

"Nana Meg puts on airs like she's the Queen of Sheba!" my mother loved to complain. To me she was a woman who knew how to shop, dye her hair pink-blonde, and polish her long, manicured nails. With each highball, her laugh got harsher and louder and her Irish brogue became more apparent. Four other grandchildren in Florida shared her heart, though they rarely visited.

And now her life-mate, my gentle grandfather, blew out his last birthday candles at the age of eighty in the hospital. He was skeletal and yellow. A rotten odor emanated from each labored breath. Cigarettes would never become my habit, and why, even after Nana Meg sobbed over his casket she continued to smoke, was a mystery to me. Their only daughter and their favorite niece would both die of throat cancer from smoking. To this day, the smell, expense, and look of anyone smoking cigarettes is repulsive to me. Whenever someone lights a cigarette, I flee the tainted air around me.

Dad had smoked cigarettes given gratis in the Army. But he quit the day he heard that the Surgeon General had found an unequivocal connection between smoking cigarettes and cancer. What smarts and willpower he had for quitting cold turkey! Even before knowing how difficult it was to overcome nicotine addiction, his decisive strength sank into his little girl's memory.

***

As hard as it was saying goodbye to my dying grandfather, I loved my maternal grandma the most.

Nana Marie and Grandpa Karl owned and micro-managed a huge German bakery in Philadelphia. My earliest memory of them was akin to winning the golden ticket to the Willie Wonka factory. This only grandchild received anything she wished for in that bakery. Wafts of warm, buttery sugar cookies, chocolate nuts, and cinnamon streusel emanated from gleaming glass rows of confection cases.

"Mom, you will ruin her dinner with that jelly donut!" my mom would protest.

"Shud up," my grandmother would reply, silencing her own daughter in her exotic accent. "She gits anyting she vants ven she comes to see her nana."

In those moments, Mother was rightfully put in her place, as I rocked back on my heels and raised my eyebrows. I was Nana Marie's to spoil and could do no wrong in her kind and loving eyes.

Even today, entering a bakery causes me to salivate and have trouble narrowing my choices while recalling the days when towers of white boxes tied up with thick, white string accompanied me home. Pop Karl took me into his working basement and showed me how he flipped the dough speedily into pretzels, cut out diamond-shaped buttery cinnamon cookies, or iced his dark chocolate signature torte. The aromas of butter, yeast, and vanilla still transport me there. The hard work of this scrimping couple resulted in the purchase of both my parents' and my first homes. When I learned later in life that Karl was not my biological grandpa, it made no difference to me. With no kids of his own, he loved me, my mom, and my nana all the more.

While my Irish grandma downplayed her Irishness, my German grandparents steeped me in their traditions, introducing me to German foods: spätzle, sauerbraten, kartoffelsalat, stollen, butterkäse, zwiebelkuchen, and of course, Schnapps, to ease my first menstrual cramps. Later came German culture: the biergartens, dirndls, edelweiss, and lessons on the hated accordion. They taught me basic words early on and expected me to study German in school.

After they sold the bakery, they moved to a brick duplex next to Nana Marie's eccentric youngest sister. Whenever we visited my grandparents, a German feast awaited us with veggies and yellow marigolds freshly picked from Nana's modest garden. She heaped food onto her blue willow china, and we ate with fancy polished silverware. Grandpa Karl would inevitably come home from his part-time baking job a bit tipsy from his stop at a beer hall. Nana berated him with German foul words flying. This bickering was simply the prelude to their unique love song.

Saying goodbye to Nana Marie elicited unbridled tears and promises to write letters, as she was the relative who gave me unconditional love and affection, the one I'd miss the most.

***

My college years never came close to the fun, carefree years of high school. My mother controlled the purse strings tightly and threw the five-thousand-dollar yearly tuition in my face.

My partial scholarship wasn't good enough for her. The first roommate with whom I was "matched" was a chain-smoking lesbian. My scholarship required me to work as kitchen staff through my first year. "Poor Protestant" might as well have been tattooed on my high forehead amidst those of the mostly Jewish students from wealthy families around me. Scraping food off of cafeteria trays made me want to escape from the posh campus. My skin crawled every time I had to work with all that garbage slop.

Things got better when I landed a spot on the cheerleading team in college. More importantly, being on the team provided me with invitations to rugby keg parties. One of the lusting, beastly rugby players there promptly seduced, then dumped me. My infatuation with this blue-eyed hulk of a rich, spoiled stud threw me into my first real depression.

Yet the saddest memory of my freshman year was my parents' decision to euthanize my dog, Boots. My earliest memory of Boots was at age two when Dad brought home an adorable mixed-breed puppy. Resembling a fox terrier, Boots was light brown with all four feet looking as though he had been dipped in white paint to mid-calf. My constant companion for the next seventeen years, he slept at the foot of my bed. Though trustworthy amongst people, he could be aggressive around other dogs. He also chased every passing car in front of our home. He successfully begged for leftovers from the school cooks while waiting for me to get out of school. It was a short trot from the back of our land to the kitchen. These ladies were on a first name basis with Boots. I was his Lady, and he was my Tramp, with the same taste for cold pasta.

Mom and Dad rang me on the only hall phone of my dorm floor to tell me he was gone. When I returned home after that semester, the house felt tomb-like without my dog's presence. He had been my substitute sibling, my companion, my teddy bear. Boots taught me that a home was incomplete without a dog.

***

When I went home on my next break, I learned that Mom knew I had sought out a gynecologist to prevent me from repeating Sharon's frightening experience. She greeted me with this unexpected barb: "We got an anonymous note in the mail saying you visited a doctor for birth control. We didn't send you to college to be a whore."

My body tensed to ward off nausea.

It was apparent that my leering roommate, with whom I had no commonalities, had sent an anonymous note to my folks. She had only fueled their closed-mindedness and my rebellion.

This betrayal was offset by landing the lead in a musical, *The Menaechmi*. I played a bikini-clad madame named Erotium in Ancient Greece. Maintaining high grades in a tough double-major while working and acting in my freshman year was a testament to my persistence.

***

The college matched me with another roommate in my sophomore year. I had nothing in common with her, either. Instead, my best pal was a cheerleader named Sheila, my first black friend. She told me of her desire to study abroad in London. Coincidentally at this time, my European roots called to me via a program with Schiller College in London. Sheila would become my roommate at the start of my junior year with my plan to then transfer to Strasbourg, France, for the second semester. My theater study would provide transferable credits and cost less than my present college tuition, so my folks were all for the experience. I applied and was accepted over the summer due to my excellent grades.

***

Aside from our family trip to Maine with Sharon, vacations had been limited to short stays to the Jersey shore. My great Aunt Margie and Uncle Albert were childless. Because Dad was their favorite nephew, they adored me. They rented a block of hotel rooms in Avalon next to a building in the form of a giant elephant. Strolling the boardwalk, chewing on salt-water taffy, and jumping over waves with Dad was as thrilling as vacations got. Flying was reserved for the wealthy. For my twelfth birthday, my great aunt Marjorie gave me a small, brown birthday book. The page for my birthday said, "You are talented in the arts. Someday you will have the opportunity to travel the world."

Was this plan to study theater arts abroad what that fortune had meant all these years?

My mother contacted my second cousins in England and Germany to tell them when to expect me. Mom gave her usual lecture on manners and pulling my own weight as a guest in their homes. My super cheapo economy flight took me from Kennedy Airport to Iceland, then Luxembourg. From there, I took a train to the English Channel, a ferry to another train to London, and finally rode the tube to my flat in Maida Vale. This two-day trip with no sleep made falling into bed easy on the third floor of a tall, white, manor-house flat. I was nearly as comatose as I was years ago during my blackberry brandy adventure at Villanova University.

***

London in 1975 was hip, vibrant, and liberating. I eagerly explored every section, first with Sheila and later with Hans. Hans was the prototype for the Arian Youth of The Reich. Tall, muscular, blond, blue-eyed, and charming, he was a star of my acting class, and I caught his eye on the first day we attended school. He called me "*mein kleiner engel*," or "my little angel," and for my entire semester abroad, he was a lover who doted on me. He attended school at the favor of his billionaire uncle who owned the entirety of Schiller College. Hans wanted to show me all of Europe in the most exciting way—with our thumbs out on city and country roads. His travel plans left me breathless with anticipation.

But first came a visit with my paternal British cousin, Peggy, and her husband, Peter, from Henley on the Thames River. They were warm and inviting with no stiff upper lips. I spent holidays and breaks with them during the London semester. They welcomed me as family with their historied culture and huge home-cooked feasts. Peggy's mother and Dad's mother were sisters, born in Ireland. But this great aunt of mine had remained in Ireland, had married a Brit, and had been disowned by her parents, my great-grandparents. My father had reestablished the family connection as a soldier in London during World War II.

They drove me far south to a ferry that took me across the English Channel to board a train that took me to my maternal great aunt Klara, her son Martin, and Martin's wife, Miriam of Schorndorf, Germany. Klara's asthma necessitated an inhaler. Her breathy German was too fast to comprehend, but communication improved through my immersion. They all lived together in a duplex, obsessed with order and scheduling to the point of nerdiness. Perhaps this was part of seeing a culture different from my own, experiencing the sights and sounds of the land my grandparents left behind for a better life at the start of the century. Klara and my nana were sisters, born in Germany. I had heard a lot about the Fatherland.

My father was drafted into the army at age nineteen. He trained as a machine gunner and paratrooper and was dropped into the French countryside on D-Day. His parachute caught on a hedgerow of brambles, saving him from a drowning death below on the flooded plain. Three days later, he was captured by German forces and spent the remainder of the war in prison camps. He quickly mastered German and became a translator for his prison mates. Although he suffered through shrapnel wounds, frostbite, dysentery, and meager rations, the elderly prison guards treated him with compassion and fairness throughout his captivity. He returned from the war to a family who had been told he had died. His father gladly welcomed him as an apprentice in his plumbing business in a section of Philadelphia ironically known as Germantown.

One of Dad's friends invited him to a sorority picnic for singles. The picnic had a twist. The men would view slabs of steak and choose their meat. Then they would meet their blind date who brought that particular cut. While going down the line with other bachelors, Dad said, "*Ich hoffe das Fleisch kommt mit der Frau mit den grossten Titten.*"

This meant he hoped the steak he chose accompanied a woman with big breasts. He chose the steak belonging to my mother. She was thin with long dark hair and proportional breasts. She had a European look, à la Ingrid Bergman. Mom was drawn to his Errol Flynn looks. Dad thought the date went well until she told him, in German, she hoped he was not disappointed he did not get the steak belonging to Miss Big Boobs. He begged for a second date to take her to a dance. There, he dropped his cockiness and fell hard for his Marie. He gave her a yellow rose for her hair at the start of the date. He proposed that night, whereupon her first answer was to laugh at his bravado. Yellow roses were forever her favorite.

Mom had been trained as a business teacher but taught full-time for only two years. A nervous woman, she never handled stress well and was content to stay at home with her only child, one she had waited to mother for nearly six years after marrying Dad in 1949. He was then a full-fledged plumber working alongside his father, the master plumber. Dad was content except for two facts: one, Mom felt he should take advantage of the GI bill and earn a degree to teach his trade, and two, my Irish grandma, Meg and my German grandma, Marie never got along well together.

This was because Nana Meg underpaid my father, whereas Marie was generous to the couple with profits from their German bakery. Indeed, if Dad had earned a fair wage, my parents would have had a more well-to-do life with a plumbing business serving the booming suburbs. Dad's fate was to be played between three scrapping hens, forever trying to please them all!

As it was, Dad loved the intellectual challenge of college and wanted most of all to please his new wife. After he earned his degree, he acquired a job at Dobbins Vo-Tech School in Philadelphia. He taught the plumbing trade to young men who went on to have a lucrative lifetime trade. Dad's parents were not at all pleased that his new German bride had steered their only son away from the family business, persuading him to become a teacher over a tradesman.

Now, decades later, my parents were not happy to hear that a strapping German was taking their daughter off on a hitchhiking adventure through Europe. Hans and I first traveled north to Blackpool, in England, and then to Scotland. We made our way through the Lake District to Edinburgh, to the charming Kingussie village, then to Loch Ness. There we found a local pub on the shoreline where I suddenly found myself ridiculously naïve at twenty years of age and the only female surrounded by a roomful of old Scotsmen and one young German.

"Where can we go to spot the Loch Ness monster?" I asked the crusty pub patriarch.

"Aye, Lassie, I kin shew ya whar the monster is!" he said as he began pulling down his crotch zipper.

An eruption of laughter exploded as we left. I covered my rosy face with my hands, as Hans told me I had set myself up perfectly for being the brunt of their little joke.

From there we took a ferry over the Irish Sea to Donegal where my ancestors were buried in graves we sought out but never found. By week's end, we had hitchhiked down to Dublin, on a ferry to Wales and back to London. The brief vacation cost us only seven dollars a day. The friendly folks we met amidst Eden-like scenery saw a carefree couple in a fog of young love.

Though my parents did not give much positive feedback in return for my letters and photos, I experienced a memorable English Christmas in Henley. Jean, Peggy's daughter, and her two toddlers joined Peggy and Peter. Then we spent a week with Hans's newly divorced parents in a small German berg. There we learned that Hans's uncle forbade his transfer to Strasbourg with me. Once I was on the college campus, a sense of bad karma enveloped me.

The campus was built first as a French estate, which became a Nazi headquarters. Two miles from the edge of the city, it looked like a massive castle. But its many cold, dark rooms within accommodated the students, dormitory style. The students and locals depressed me with their incredible snobbery. Friendships had been established that first semester, with no place for me. Pining for Hans, my plan was to hitchhike back to London and surprise him before the semester began. My guardian angel never worked so hard as throughout this impetuous trek.

Two kind students offered to drive me to Brussels, leaving at midnight. We nearly arrived, thirty kilometers south, when their car broke down. Just before this mishap, the police stopped us for not having headlights on. Back on the road, the driver sighed, noticeably relieved. He opened his glove box to reveal a huge stash of marijuana, which could have resulted in our imprisonment in a foreign jail that night. After leaving my fellow students with their pot and their problem, I hitched one long, uneventful hitchhike ride to the ferry terminal, then I traveled across the channel, whereupon four young Iranian men picked me up after dark. My instincts had me on edge, but that guardian angel whispered in my ear to show them a diamond ring my nana had given me. I talked myself out of the danger that hung heavily in that car. "I want you to know my German fiancée is waiting for me tonight!" I cooed sweetly.

My arrival at my true love's flat was in the early morning. Hans opened the door, surely delighted to see me. Breezing right on past him to his bedroom, I found before me lying naked in his bed a familiar student from our acting class, the pudgy one with the long blonde hair and the worst actress in our class.

"*Meine kleine* angel, I didn't expect you!" he stammered.

Female eyes locked in jealous rage.

"If you don't get out of here fast, every blonde hair will be ripped out of your head," I promised aloud.

My body was reacting to pure betrayal, hyperventilating, meaning every measured word.

My, she moved fast! My wails of betrayal and his insistence that she meant nothing filled the exhausting night.

To allay his infidelity, he hitchhiked with me back to Strasbourg, where I pleaded to cancel my second semester abroad and return to New Jersey. We waved our final goodbyes at a French train station. Once again, I learned through my misery, that boys could not be trusted.

My time abroad took me back to when I played Wendy in the third grade. Flying away for a time had expanded my world, allowing me to taste cultures vastly different from what a small-town Pennsylvania girl was used to. My ancestors had left Germany, where folks ran their lives like well-oiled machines. Conversely, my Irish, now English, kin were warmly accepting of me and immersed in theater, music, and the arts during their colorful retirement. My stay had lasted long enough. A philandering Peter Pan had betrayed me. My heart needed to mend back in familiar territory. Hans's uncle saw to my full semester refund, probably relieved to dispense me far away from his Romeo nephew who would then cease hitchhiking across the continent with a foreigner.

***

With supplemental summer and January course credits at my home university under my belt, my studies continued for another year before I graduated early. For a gift, my father gave me my grandpa's clunker. No one else wanted the old, black AMC Rambler. At least I could now get jobs waitressing off-campus. This meant picking up the car at my parents' Philadelphia home and driving it back to New Jersey.

Dad had me follow him to a gas station. Raucous teenagers at a nearby gas pump attracted my attention.

"Come on Retard Boy, beg for us like a dog, and we'll give you your donut," they teased.

A teen with Down syndrome was looking hungrily at the bakery box held just above him. Dad was astounded when I sprang from my car, screaming at this urban street gang as I ran closer: "Don't you ever treat a human being like an animal. You should be ashamed of yourselves. You are monsters! Now give him the entire box of donuts! And never taunt him again! If you do, you will surely all be damned to Hell!"

I felt my body shake, wanting vengeance on all the world's bullies.

All froze, momentarily unsettled by my outburst. The victim received the slowly lowered box of donuts. Dad just wanted to get me inside of my newly acquired Rambler and away from the thugs. At that gas station, my passion for defending underdogs from brutes was ignited. I had truly felt a dopamine rush from this experience. It hinted of future career pursuits lying ahead.

***

In my senior year, my gorgeous friend Taffy came to me with a lucrative job offer—to work with her as a nude art model for a figure drawing class. It was liberating to pose, not having a stitch on, to see how artists' eyes portrayed me. There was a sublime feeling in the creative energy of artists around me, and the sixteen-dollars-an-hour wage was more than any other job paid on campus. I wanted someday to return to this creative atmosphere, but behind the easel, not in front. It sure beat slopping garbage off of trays.

***

Vernon came into my life shortly after my return from Europe. He was the star of the basketball and baseball teams, and he was a sleek black jaguar. At six feet, four inches tall, muscular, with cat eyes, he had the biggest, softest lips and the most charming smile I had ever seen. His deep, bass voice soothed me. He had a space between his front teeth, just like me, and he was a natural comic with a fabulous laugh. He was a taboo I had been warned about since I was young.

The first time I heard the h-word and the n-word was from my Irish grandmother, Meg.

"Don't you ever wear the green on St. Patty's Day! That's only worn by the crazy *harps*," she'd say. This was the regional slur used by the Irish Protestants to denote Irish Roman Catholics. "A Catholic is just an inside-out nigger, so I'm warning you never to befriend them."

My parents carried this ugly attitude forward. They were the Archie and Edith Bunker of Warrington, spouting out every derogatory term for those unlike themselves, united in bigotry.

My second memory of this divisive thinking came when my family and I were leaving our favorite restaurant in New Hope. My father saw a black man escorting a white woman to their car.

"Don't you ever do what that nigger-loving woman is doing, or you will be disowned," he said.

This little girl could only nod sadly, confused. My Sunday school lessons and American history lessons contradicted these words uttered in a lowered voice by my visibly upset father. My mother would never think of challenging his bigotry, a mouse to his lion. By this time, Dad was working on his graduate degree from the University of Pennsylvania. He carried a gun to night classes due to the gang members who prowled around parking lots at night. He painted all black people with the same broad brush. I knew, even then, my father's thinking was flawed.

I learned how during America's bicentennial year, just the sight of two people of different color in a relationship incited jealousy, disgust, anger, judgment, and hypocrisy. Vernon and I felt only peace, beauty, understanding, and unity. My parents' bigotry came from fear and ignorance.

When I told my father of my relationship with Vernon, he told others that he no longer had a daughter. So, one day I decided to drive home and introduce Vernon to just my mother, hoping she would see the good in his soul. I was dead wrong. She later phoned me at college.

"How could you bring a monkey to our home? The neighbors nearly called the police!"

"Why would they call the police?" I asked her, completely clueless.

"Because he was in front of our home!"

I was rocked with resentment toward my parents' bigotry, though decades later judgment comes from many, usually men, when they learn of this period in my life.

My most enduring college friendships were formed with another couple whose parents opposed their union. Gary was Vernon's best friend. Joy was the offspring of an Italian dad and Puerto Rican mom who endured parental judgment when *they* were young, yet when she fell in love with multiracial Gary, her parents repeated the sins of their fathers. Gary, Joy, and I remain friends to this day. Gary still claims Joy was the greatest love of his life.

***

When my Rambler died, so did my waitress job. It was time to find my first post-college job. I was hired by a large insurance company as a claims adjuster. The best part of this adventure was my company car: a 1972 white Ford Mustang Mach 1 with a baby blue interior. Ah, to have wheels again! Training would entail a six-week period at the Philadelphia Marriott hotel, then across from the iconic art museum where famed Rocky Balboa ran victoriously down the steps.

I investigated all types of claims initially. My training introduced me to spotting fraudulent workmen's compensation claims; handling homeowner's claims where the photos I had to take of burned-out trailers or water leaks provided critical documentation; and analyzing product liability claims, in which many folks were trying to prove that after ingesting or applying some product, their wrongful pain and suffering had ensued. Most of the time, though, my travels took me to intersections, mile markers, police stations, and hospitals to gather all the gory details of auto accidents.

Within six months, I got promoted to the role of court adjuster, a position that required working with lawyers on the top-money cases. The job appealed to me, because it warded off the inherent boredom of being a cog in a wheel. I found many a strange story in statements from north Jersey. A nun sued a candy bar company due to a broken denture. A diabetic blamed the loss of his leg on a topical spray. A facial dog bite scar that resulted from a child teasing a relative's pet was worth big bucks. To many naïve claimants, mine was the face of a multi-million-dollar insurance corporation. Young and pretty, I had no trouble earning their trust…and their signature on a liability release. Although it felt somewhat unethical doing this job, it never bored me that first year.

But Vernon bored me. Once we were out of the protective campus surroundings, Vernon began smoking too much weed and drinking too many beers. He did not have the same drive that my new job had instilled in me. He didn't care if he finished his degree. Why would I want a life-mate who was a pothead with lost ambition? I had been enabling him by supporting him. Plus, it was not fun to be disowned by my parents, to encounter bigotry from men shouting "nigger-lover" from their cars as they passed us on the street, or to be yelled at once by a drunken black woman for "taking one of our men away when you had no right to be lovin' on him."

The hourglass sands were dwindling between us. Reality presented me with a man who wanted to continue in a relationship, yet had flaws that could not be rectified or defended anymore. What I would forever admire is the bravery needed in relationships when there are outward differences between lovers, whether due to age, gender, race, religion, or handicaps. The lesson I carried from this relationship is that society is profoundly intolerant of relationships falling outside of the norm, despite what the media and entertainment worlds tell us.

My father had earned his master's degree in administrative education by this time. Consequently, his next job moved my parents a day's car trip away to the southwestern corner of the state. They were so angry with me that they rid themselves of all my possessions in the moving process. Gone were my saxophone, books, clothes, and memories from living and working in Warrington. Oddly, the item I missed most was a red glass apple from Mrs. C that always caught the sunlight on my windowsill. I saw one like it in a store once, but it wasn't hers.

"Oh, I sold everything in a garage sale," Mom answered blithely, when I asked what had happened to all of my things.

It occurred to me that my town was aptly named—a town of warring, with my parents. I promised myself then that I would refuse to be like them, prejudiced against all who were not like them. I wanted to be open-minded about my relationships, my evolving faith, and my career paths yet to come. I thought about Mrs. C and how I could draw inspiration from her instead on how to live my life; I had gleaned early on that Mrs. C was a woman with a much more open-minded view of the world. After all, she had been divorced.

As a consequence of this realization, I upped my correspondence with Mrs. C. She was happy to see me when I made the drive south to visit her and my nana Marie. Both of these adored women listened without judgment to the details of my life. In fact, without my asking, my maternal grandmother paid off my college loan.

Nana and I agreed to travel together at Christmas to the other end of the state to visit my parents. We flew out of Philadelphia, landed in Pittsburgh, and after we returned, my plan was to have one full day in my hometown to visit with Sharon and Mr. and Mrs. C. The events of that Christmas day are fuzzy, but the details of December 26, 1977, would forever alter my life.

CHAPTER TWO

Up to Bat

On that one day back in Warrington, my plan was first to visit my old beau Bobby, who said he now regretted our break-up, and then my best friend Sharon. But early in the day, I made a surprise visit to Mr. and Mrs. C. As soon as they opened the door, they welcomed me into a large family gathering, and the matriarch herself said it was vital that we catch up on the past year. A truly handsome, red-headed Kevin Costner look-alike approached me with a shy smile.

"Ah'm Jon Love. Mrs. C is my aunt—Mom's sister," he said with a southern drawl.

"Well, you certainly got her red hair. Love that two-tone you have going on there," I said.

His beard was auburn, and his thick straight strawberry-blond mane gleamed above me, from atop a frame that was well over six feet. His eyes were the same green-hazel hue as my own, large and round, a Scots-Irish Jesus Christ. We were immediately drawn to each other.

Mrs. C's brother snapped our photo as we blushed. Thereafter, it was as if we were alone in the room. I stood up

Bobby that evening, as he could not follow this act. Jon took me for a ride around my old neighborhood. He lit up a joint, and I took an obligatory toke. That should have been my first warning. But then, he sweetly kissed me in the parking lot of the nearby single-runway airport.

"You should know I live with someone else. His name is Vernon," I confessed.

"Do you love him?" he asked, those dreamy eyes boring into mine.

"Not after that kiss," I replied, appreciating my world and everything in it at that moment.

Before parting, we exchanged addresses and graduation photos from our wallets.

Later, Mrs. C looked me in the eye. "My dear, be careful," she cautioned.

That was my second warning. My brain should've gone into high gear with my role model sending up this red flare. Alas, she was much too late.

"I met my husband today," I told Sharon that night as I passed his photo to her.

Five weeks later, a Boeing took me south to Charlotte for the first time. Jon and I consummated our love in a dingy trailer. Who could have guessed it'd happen in a doublewide? That should have been my third warning. Soon we were shopping for my engagement ring, and within a month, he drove to New Jersey to move me and my meager belongings to North Carolina. There he found a new townhouse to appease me. The experience of young love, in a warm climate, in a sleepy southern town stretched before me. I barely understood the twang of the grocery clerks at the local Piggly Wiggly. We adopted a gray tabby we named

Liebes, meaning "love" in German. Despite having little in common besides our fondness for a cat and Jon's Aunt Peg, we frantically planned to marry on my parents' twenty-ninth anniversary, also my grandparents' anniversary. Mrs. C would become *my* Aunt Peg when I married her ever-so-handsome nephew to become Mrs. Love. What could go wrong with our plan? He was a white man from a solid Protestant family. I daydreamed often during those days leading up to our wedding, unable to think about anything else, wanting it to be perfect.

Jon had a bachelor's degree in economics from a nearby North Carolina college. He worked in a sprinkler factory and loved the slow-moving south, whereas it quickly became clear to me that I was a fish out of water. My neighbor townhouse ladies had no kids, no jobs, and seemed content to tan and get drunk by the community pool. The cultural chasm between urban north and rural south was deep and vast.

One night, we went out to a jazz club. While Jon became increasingly drunk, I asked a musician there if he played at weddings, only to be hastily pulled from the club and driven home, where Jon smashed a bottle against a brick wall near my face. He had worked himself into a jealous rage over nothing and I angrily told him so when he sobered up. Later, Jon told me he would stay away from hard liquor and that he would give up cigarettes for me, too. Still, despite *this* crystal-clear warning, we kept moving forward with wedding plans. Jon wrote a letter to my parents requesting a healing of our breach, telling them of our impending union. We ultimately gained our family's approval by planning the ceremony in Warrington.

To say that this romance seemed to be happening quickly is an understatement.

***

Though I had experienced a torrid romance with Vernon, he would never be accepted by my family and he was not breaking any achievement records. Vernon had sobbed when I ended our relationship, but our breakup was in my best interest. Jon was a man whose German-Irish genes matched my own. Better yet, his aunt, whom he also adored, was my own adopted mother figure. He was proclaiming his enduring love for me and he was so easy on the eyes.

Those eyes—large, round, and puppy-like. His hair was leonine and truly the most beautiful red shade I'd ever seen on a man. Yet, he was shy and sweet, unaware of his good looks because he had always been compared to his smarter, thinner, older brother, who at the time had a respected military career, a beautiful wife, and two children.

The dawning realization that his intellect did not quite match my own was overshadowed by the adoration of a handsome man from a family of which I yearned to be a member. Besides, my heart melted when he played his guitar and sang with me…sweet southern folk tunes in harmony for Mrs. C, who would now be known forevermore as *my* Aunt Peg.

At least my grandmas were happy for me. Nana Marie bought me my sleek lace wedding gown, one that I found in a bridal magazine. She, more than Mom, assisted in planning a ceremony in a little country church made of stone, with a reception for sixty guests at a posh inn nearby. My mother clearly did not share in the excitement of my wedding planning.

"I have doubts about Jon," Mom declared five days before our wedding.

"Well, do tell, Mom." I felt my body temperature rise, my neck stiffen, my head throb.

"I'm concerned about his conceit, his lack of drive, and you obviously loving him more than he loves you."

"Jon is not, in fact, conceited, just very quiet. And he is very handsome," I said through gritted teeth, wanting to flee.

"Well, I don't find him handsome! But I want to know if he likes me." So this wedding was all about her.

When I relayed her question to Jon, he said simply, "I think she's just a little bit nuts."

A wedding photographer captured me walking down the aisle with a terrified look on my twenty-three-year-old face, walking to stand with my bridesmaids and best friends, Sharon and Nancy. Perhaps the fear I felt was a premonition of our camping honeymoon that Jon planned soon thereafter in Canada during the rainiest, buggiest August ever. I despised camping and begged in Trois-Rivieres to spend just one night in a cheap motel. That night felt like a luxurious spa retreat. Nana Marie gifted us with Jon's dream vehicle, a green Jeep, as a wedding present, which we drove to our planned destinations. Off-roading was the inspiration for our Canadian trek. Spotting a moose by the Bay of Fundy was my biggest thrill of the entire honeymoon.

***

Despite Mom's misgivings about Jon, she wanted us to be closer to her and Dad, and she persuaded us to move nearer to them. Jon got a job managing a loan office. This company expected a manager who took no pity on those who defaulted on high-interest loans. Soft-spoken Jon hated conflict, skirting his own bills.

My own professional life drifted during that time. For a while, I modeled for a college figure drawing class, this time in my bikini. Then I worked as an insurance investigator with two independent firms, first in an office within walking distance and then for a Pittsburgh firm, working out of my home office. Once I investigated the death of a farmer's frozen cow shot by an errant arrow, but the usual calls were to take photos of long-haul trucking accidents along nearby interstate highways.

My main duty as an investigator was to take signed statements of claimants. In the winter of 1979, a new case took me to the tiny village of Paris, Pennsylvania, in below-freezing weather to take a statement from a man named Robbie. He met me in a neck brace, obviously faking injury, but what drew me in was his beautiful family: his wife, Liz; their baby girl; and an obedient black Doberman named Dillon. Robbie told me about Devil's Den Rock Formation, a nearby place to go off-roading.

Three days later, Jon and I found ourselves deep in the Devil's Den, stuck in a frozen mud puddle. We walked over icy hills to a house where folks were trusting enough to allow us to call a neighbor for rescue. We learned what a winch was and invested in one. The next day, we went to Robbie and Liz's home where Liz warmly welcomed us. Jon bonded with Robbie, who helped to retrieve our Jeep. Liz and I became lifelong friends, all over a faked pain in the neck by a man who went on to become a *real* pain in the neck to my sister-friend.

In the first year of our marriage, I convinced Jon to audition with me for *Our Town* at a community theater. We landed the lead roles as George and Emily. My dad landed the role of George's father, as he'd acted in community theater when he was our age. This would begin a decade of acting together in plays where we met our closest friends.

Sex during the early years of any marriage is usually blissful, but playing lovers on stage spiced things up even more. Going off of birth control also amped up the excitement level.

***

Jon's mom and step-dad moved to Florida, and we visited them for the first time as a married couple in 1979. There, we told them of our recent discovery. Jon had had a seizure at an office party and following the subsequent tests he had endured, he was diagnosed with grand mal epilepsy. The doctor advised Jon to take Dilantin and drink moderately. His parents drank Scotch every day at "cocktail hour." His mother gladly supplied Jon with eight drinks on our last day there, oblivious to the doctor's advice relayed to her.

To the best of my memory, this argument ensued during our ride home:

"I feel worried because you drink so much," I said, broaching the topic with an "I" statement, enabling him to deflect the criticism to my feeling, rather than on his action.

"I will stop drinking to get you to stop nagging. Just don't ask me to give up my weed."

"You want me to get high with you when I don't want to. Can't we live a clean life?"

"Who made you God? Maybe you should have married a minister," he retorted.

"Just maybe, God doesn't want us to weaken our bodies by getting buzzed so much, especially when on Dilantin with a brain wave disorder. Our health should come first."

"Don't you dare try to take away my weed," he said, as if he had met his Waterloo.

"You actually sound panicky at the thought. Can we just *try* being clean for a while?"

He agreed, for a time, after much crying on my part and screaming on his. This argument was the beginning of a ten-year pattern of fighting, during which his drinking and drugging never ended.

***

Wanting to get pregnant, I lived healthily. In the fall of our second year of marriage, we learned that we were indeed expecting. We saved enough money to go on a cruise to the Bahamas. I quit my job in the insurance field forever. We prepared to be parents in a slightly larger rented apartment in the same small town. Aunt Peg was to become a great aunt to our child. In my spare time, I sewed a whole wardrobe of baby clothes. I again attempted to mend fences with my parents, as we awaited the baby and our restored relationship seemed to be a healthier one.

We attended a Marriage Encounter, a healing weekend in Butler, Pennsylvania, to connect as a Christian couple. There, we met Ken and Ellen, and at the end of the weekend, they told us they had prayed for us. Ken was the pastor of a small church in our town. We soon joined the church, and Ken and Ellen became our close friends. We hoped for a beautiful little girl like their toddler Sarah. Whenever we visited them, my longing gaze watched lovely Sarah at play. I didn't realize at the time how much I would soon need the spiritual comfort that these friends provided.

***

Early in my pregnancy, I told my doctor of my moderate morning sickness.

"A Bendectin pill every day will help. It is just like taking a vitamin," he said.

Trusting this doctor, who trusted the FDA, was the worst mistake of my entire life.

In the summer of 1980, after a long transition labor, Danielle was delivered with forceps.

The doctor did not hold her up to me immediately. Instead, he prepared me by saying, "There seems to be a problem."

He then explained that she had a cleft lip, a cleft palate, and a missing finger before letting me see her. Seeing her face put me into shock. My emotions flatlined. I robotically watched Jon sob over my hospital bed. Danielle could not nurse. Feeding her with an eyedropper caused her to choke. In the days that followed, prescription pills dried up my breast milk.

With each day came more devastating news. My world was spinning. I remember hearing, "She appears to have brain damage." Then, "She appears to be blind." And finally, "She was born with a hole in her heart. We are transferring her to Children's Hospital downtown."

Pastor Ken came to the hospital and baptized her. He was the only visitor I wanted to see.

Every morning, upon awakening, I felt a weight descend on my chest as if a heavy iron lay there. My body was transitioning from a dreamland to the reality of our baby, who was dying.

When it was time to take her home, I was averse to it. The medical staff told me she would turn blue at some point and die, due to her continually weakening heart. I could not face such a morbid situation, watching her die. She stayed at the hospital and I went home, and yet I heard her cries while listening to the radio or when I was driving my car... auditory hallucinations. My depression was so great that my sanity was eroding.

A month after her birth, Danielle died at the hospital. My prayer for relief had been answered. I believe with my entire being, however, that I will meet her again, whole and beautiful in Jesus's arms upon my arrival in Heaven. I am just as certain that she would have been beautiful on Earth, were it not for some unknown cause.

I wasn't sure what the cause was. It became my mission to find out what robbed us of parenthood. My pregnancy was a time of deep bonding with Jon. We romanticized and idealized our relationship, dreaming of how our perfect baby would make us three. Now this tragic loss was all the more earth-shattering for our marriage. We'd mourn the loss in very different ways.

My hormones were screaming to nurture. Although we heard stories of babies born with issues, we believed it could never happen to us. My shock and depression changed me forever. I could not depend on Jon to fix my heartache.

I needed a personal God. I began my own faith journey to answer what every grieving mother asks: "Why did this happen to me?"

Because Jon did not seek to heal spiritually, but rather by means of alcohol and pot, our relationship became more fractured. The trauma of losing a first baby never heals. It affected my parenting and my overprotection of children and grandchildren to come. I still begin each daily prayer with, "Lord of love, Giver of life!"

Pastor Ken tried to help us through our grief with these assuring words of theological wisdom: "When folks tell you it was God's will, tell them kindly, it definitely was not. Jesus weeps *with* you. Some form of evil caused this, not anything of God."

As much comfort as this advice gave us, my parents caused us pain when they told us marijuana surely was the cause. I had long ago stopped smoking, but Jon still grew his own plants in our mountaintop garden. Still, we confided in our geneticist. We were relieved when he concluded, "Random mutations caused this, not marijuana. You have a green light to try again."

***

As 1981 began our third year of marriage, we needed to get far away from the memories of this time and place. An opportunity came along that delighted Jon, a former Eagle Scout. He would manage a loan office in the middle of rural West Virginia—in those days, truly a hillbilly heaven.

Nana Marie generously gave us a down payment on our first home, a log chalet atop a rolling lot of ten acres. The remote crossroads near our home were twelve miles from any store, doctor, or post office. Though the fields and forests were pristine, our heating source was a wood-fueled, forced air stove and a two-foot-long baseboard electric heater in the bathroom. Envision Eva Gabor in the sitcom *Green Acres*.

This was a whole new, odd way of life. The only way to acclimate was with the help of our neighbors, Mel and Sally and Bucky and Hazel, with whom we shared our dirt road. Our other new companion was Schatzie, our beautiful red Doberman puppy. Her first home was in dog paradise. She ran free with our new friends' yellow lab and Irish setter. No fences separated our land. We were introduced to a whole community of "fer-en-ers," or those who hailed from middle class suburbia, making a life homesteading in the rural countryside. We joined a food co-op and partied on weekends with artists and musicians in our age group.

Soon I was pregnant again and everyone assured me all would be well *this* time. Unfortunately, there was no gynecologist practicing in the county for this high-risk patient. I traveled more than two hours to the state capital to be under the care of young, handsome, and brilliant Dr. Paul.

Despite others' well-meaning placating, my pregnancy ended with a sixteen-week miscarriage. While I was bleeding profusely, Sally, who resembled a Swedish, hippy midwife, raced me hours away to the big city women's hospital. Though we were devastated, Dr. Paul told us not to give up, as did our minister from our new tiny church, which was seventeen miles away over the mountain roads.

My refuge became my deepening faith, singing in a small church choir, and acting in community theater. Jon was doing his best managing his loan office while making friends with his employees.

To work as a substitute teacher for the county, I studied a prep manual for the National Teachers Exam, geared toward those who had studied a teaching block in college. Soon, I aced the test. My strong work ethic landed me a stint teaching gifted elementary students. Even better, the curriculum was of my own choosing. I taught German, botany, and the arts…my interests.

Finally, in the winter of '81, I was pregnant at the same time as my neighbor Hazel, who resembled a young Dolly Parton with frosted hair. We laughed and prayed together through these shared tense months of pregnancy. We dressed in long red underwear to play Tweedledee and Tweedledum in neighbor Sally's annual summer solstice celebration. Amniocentesis bore out that we had a healthy girl. All was going smoothly until Jon was fired for not being hard enough on his deadbeat clients and his employees. But then, one of our few friends with local connections told Jon to apply for a supervisor position at a training workplace for disabled adults. He began this job just two days before I was to give birth.

***

Early in this third pregnancy, I researched the drug Bendectin and began reading the Association for Bendectin Children newsletter, which taught me about lawsuits against the drug company. Getting money for the death of a child is unethical to me, as there is no earthly value for such a loss. Yet, I told everyone I knew of the FDA cover-up and the greedy payoffs by Richardson-Merrell, the pharmaceutical company now known as Marion Merrell Dow, outlined in a November 1980 article by Mark Dowie and Carolyn Marshall called

"The Bendectin Cover-Up" in *Mother Jones* magazine. From the moment I learned of the potential dangers of Bendectin, I drank natural peppermint tea to overcome any morning sickness. Nothing artificial went into my body. I washed every vegetable and prayed to be blessed with the healthy baby girl inside of me.

***

On July 22, beautiful, blonde, blue-eyed Jessa was born. Never were there so many happy tears and so much joy in our hearts. Life was complete. Our prayers had been answered. Our relatives made the journey to see this adored baby baptized, with Jon's only childless sister acting as her godmother, though I barely knew anything of her or her faith.

The kinfolk expressed consternation as to why we chose to live so far out in the sticks, but this was paradise in Jon's eyes. When I asked if living there might be temporary, he led me by my hand to the back field and made me lay down. He crossed my arms over my chest and said, "I'll make sure you're buried here. We will never leave this place."

A sour taste came to my mouth, and I thought to myself, *"You may be buried here, but I'll be damned if I will be also."*

He knew of my discomfort, but he didn't care about the hardships of raising children here, twelve miles from medical help, through biting winters, far from family. This was Jon's mindset, living the life of his glory days as an Eagle Scout, camping out in the wilderness permanently.

CHAPTER THREE
Squeeze Play

Winters were challenging in the middle of nowhere, when we had to lug our groceries home a half-mile uphill in Jessa's red wagon or by a sled in the snow. The muddy ruts in our private dirt road made it impassable. This could have been averted with a small share of family money passed down from my parents. And where might this money have come from?

Nana Meg passed away peacefully in Florida soon after visiting us to see Jessa. Though wealthy, my aunt Eve coerced Dad into giving his half of the inheritance to her. She justified it by saying she cared for them at their end, yet Dad saw to their needs for most of their lives. Dad hated family conflict. So, she then carted away every one of my grandparents' possessions. Mom was furious, but her actions should have been no surprise. Aunt Eve was not into sharing.

While looking out of our bedroom window at the falling snow, Jessa napping nearby, a memory took me back to my fourteenth summer. It began with my first airplane ride from Philadelphia to Ft. Lauderdale. Mom and Dad celebrated their twentieth anniversary in Hawaii, and my Aunt Eve and

Uncle Cal were charged with my care for a two-week period. My four cousins had been strangers, but they were family to Dad. I had a crush on my cousin Lee…tall, handsome, tanned. Gayle was a year younger than me. She breathed heavily through her mouth and tried bossing us around in big-sister mode. Mark was Lee's cute tag-a-long brother with a lazy eye. The youngest, Lori, was coddled and whiny due to minor complications of her premature birth.

A few days into my visit, we all went to a baseball game of Lee's. His team captain wanted to meet me. When my aunt heard I'd taken a short walk with him away from the field, she became Cruella de Vil, whisking the family into her car and screaming at me the entire way home. As she ranted on, I thought, *"All I did was talk to him, yet every day who does your ironing while you and Cal 'nap?'"* (Note to self: The gators can keep Florida—and all its skeeters, snakes, spiders, geezers, and high humidity.)

So, there I was, watching snow fall and hatching a plan to find money to fix our road. I had to better my education in order to gain more income. Living in the boonies came with costs.

***

My master's degree in counseling began with a unique night class field trip to the Weston Hospital for the Mentally Ill. In the run-down institution's ward for the low-functioning, the staff had laid out thin mattresses on rickety metal frames in cold, tiled, gray rooms. Men and women wandered about, either wanting to touch us or staring vacantly ahead. It reeked. Most of them were naked because they would continually rip off their clothes if dressed. I had seen dogs boarded more humanely. I would someday aid in the closure of this place, though even at that time, such an environment was unimaginable and certainly not open to the general public.

On the day of this field trip, a check arrived from Nana Marie to pay off our mortgage. Nana told me not to tell my parents, as they'd be jealous of me getting *any* of her funds. This made no sense. When I was nine, we moved a mile north of our first home in Warrington. Mom convinced Nana to buy her a home with fieldstone facing and a fireplace, an apple and blueberry orchard out back, and giant shade trees anchoring Dad's rope hammock. After the purchase of this home, my grandparents visited more often, along with Dad's Air Force Reserve buddies. They joined us for picnics on hot summer nights with Hire's root beer, buttery corn on the cob, and grilled burgers—treats that screamed, "School's out for summer!" Mom gladly accepted my grandmother's generosity to buy her an upgraded house. Why wouldn't she want to see my life made easier in the same manner? Apparently, Mom was not into sharing, either.

When Mom took over her own mother's finances, Mom called me in a fury and said, "We had to wait five years more than you to have *our* first mortgage paid off by Nana."

I thought back to when Jon had been unemployed. We asked Mom only once for help, to buy groceries for a week. She had sent just twenty-five dollars. Nana Marie, who became outraged when she found out about this, told me, "Don't you ever ask them for another dollar!"

I vowed then, if fortune ever came my way, I'd be generous toward family and friends. I told myself it was only money.

The more important things in life were love and marriage. And just how were those things going?

***

The year 1982 ended with a small party at our home where Jon vomited his liquor. My journal entry recorded, "The pattern: He overdrinks, gets nasty, makes me cry, then apologizes." Naivety prevented me from seeing that he was an alcoholic. A mere week later, he went to a neighborhood party, got drunk, and hit me afterward, bruising my nursing breast.

He swore off alcohol again. I finally confided in Aunt Peg that I feared for our marriage.

Then, a feud arose on our mountain between the families sharing our road over rights of way in a deed. Our two nearest neighbors screamed at each other and did not speak for years after. As friends to both, we were caught in the middle and attempted to mediate their inane Hatfield-McCoy feud.

At least it took us away from our own battles for a time—until a summer wedding when Jon was drunk and almost ran us off the road before the wheel was under my control. On the drive home, he cursed me and told me to leave him. The next day, he swore off alcohol. How many times had he done this by now? It was getting to be an old pattern that continued *ad nauseam*. And it wasn't just the booze he craved.

Jon harbored an obsession with his pot plants. If I mentioned any of my concerns about the risk involved with keeping such plants, he got moody and nasty, letting me know of my status—obviously beneath pot. He thought nothing of taking our toddler Jessa to a local hippie hangout, getting high, having a few beers, and driving home to sleep it off with little thought for her safety. This kind of behavior put me into mama grizzly bear mode, defending my cubs.

Soon after this argument, Jon and I landed leading roles again, this time in a Halloween production of *Dracula*. But I took a hiatus from rehearsals when Jessa developed tonsillitis with a fever of more than 105 degrees. When we picked up Jon at work to rush her to the pediatrician, he cursed me loudly before getting in the car, somehow seeing her tonsillitis as my fault. He later refused to apologize, so I escaped with Jessa to my parents. It was five days before his apology came, bringing us home once again. This was in our fifth year of marriage.

A getaway came about with Sharon to my tenth-year high school reunion. Jessa experienced her first airplane flight to New Jersey, where Sharon picked us up on her way home to Warrington. That trip also provided a chance to visit my dear nana Marie and my in-laws. And when we reunited with Aunt Peg several days later, she gave Jessa dozens of the finest children's books available. Jon drove himself to meet us for a wedding in Delaware, where I danced the night away… while he drank the night away…again.

Leaving the suburbs and returning to the discomforts of living in the depressing, poor hills of Appalachia proved to be more and more difficult. First, our minister was forced to resign from our rural church where Jessa was baptized. The "woman preacher" had never really been welcome. Second, Jon's latest drunken binge sent me into a depression that had me thinking of divorcing him for the first time. But how could I be so cruel as to take away Jessa, the love and joy of our lives? Meanwhile, my pal Liz visited to confide in me that her husband, Robbie, beat her and that she was preparing to leave him. Maybe I could indeed do the same? If only I didn't want sex with Jon, my decision would be easier.

A routine blood test by Dr. Paul confirmed that the hormone responsible for my sex drive was at 150 percent. This explained my need to be physically loved by Jon; still, even *that* was ebbing. There's an old song about a "natural high." Do women really want to share their most intimate moments with drugs and alcohol? The smells alone are off-putting. Was it vain of me to want to be able to arouse my husband without the aid of pot and booze?

***

Life seesawed from sad thoughts to wonderful surprises. At the start of 1984, Jon and I played opposite leads once more in a local theater production of *Guys and Dolls,* where we sang love songs to each other. And I began a fine-art class at a nearby college, carpooling every Friday with our friend, Will. He and his wife were friends Jon and I had known since our move to our log home amidst the Appalachian Mountains.

Will was an artist from New York City who had settled with his family in a small town. He was the opposite of Jon in every way. He was short and muscular, half Italian and half Norwegian, with dark curly hair. Suave and confident, he was the life of any party. He had an open marriage, and he set his sights on me when we first met after his performance in a play.

Will was a gifted sculptor, and he soon learned of my past as an art model. He asked me to model for him in exchange for some sketched portraits. We attended the same parties, where we would dance, eyes locked. Johnny Depp and Sharon Stone would play us in my mind's movie.

Like me, he was an extrovert married to an introvert. Our mates soon saw that our chemistry was electrifying. During that time, I wrote in my journal: "What an exciting ego trip to be desired by him. The control is always there, mixed with feelings of anxiety and doubt…no consummation but certainly emotional escalation."

Will treated me like a princess. He was kind, adoring, and lavished me with sexy words. This contrasted with Jon's treatment of me. Jon saw me as a barrier to getting buzzed. What kept me at bay was the desire to give Jessa something that had been missing in my life—a sibling. Living so far out in the country, she deserved a childhood less lonely than mine was.

I have an early memory from the 1950s, from realizing that all my friends had siblings. I had asked my father, "How come I don't have a brother or a sister?"

"Mommy was told by the doctor it's too dangerous," he'd replied. "She only has one kidney that works."

My grandmothers later told me that they questioned this reasoning. It seemed to us that Mom was just too nervous to have another child. Perhaps since she was an only child, it was her norm to bear only one child. Her pain tolerance was low. She often told me of my difficult birth.

But I was determined to get pregnant again, by my husband. That determination paid off when we learned we were expecting, and amniocentesis confirmed another healthy baby girl.

Shortly after learning of my pregnancy, this conversation with Jon transpired:

"Did you know Will has been trying to seduce me for years now, and I have resisted?" I asked.

"I have no problem with an open marriage," he replied. "If that is what you want, then go for it."

What I had needed to hear was, "I'm proud of you for resisting," or "Hell no, you're my woman."

To make things worse, Jon then told me about a chorus girl in *Guys and Dolls* he wanted to have an affair with. It became clear: Jon wanted to open our marriage pronto for his own desires.

Now that I was already pregnant by Jon, Will was irresistible. I loved two men. With full permission from Jon, though I knew it wasn't right, Will became my addiction, my highest high. Chicago came out with a song, "Hard Habit to Break." The song seemed to sum up my addiction. I never felt more beautiful, and as lovers, they made me feel like a goddess in very different ways.

During this time, Jon seemed to try harder to be a doting husband. Perhaps it was in knowing that I was desired by another, a man whom Jon admired and enjoyed being around. But it was Jessa who bonded us in love, and she was a delight. We adored her. At age three, she excelled in all areas of learning, reading dozens of flashcard words long before preschool. And she was so darned cute with her platinum, curly locks and big, blue eyes. Would I love my new baby this much?

CHAPTER FOUR
Strike One

On August 22, Dr. Paul delivered Fern, sealing his status as hero when he reached inside of me to unwrap her umbilical cord from around her then-pale, blue throat. And yes, I loved my new baby fiercely.

Though blonde like Jessa, Fern's eyes were vivid green. She was smaller than her sister with an easier disposition, surely due to a less-nervous mother. More happy tears flowed over a second gorgeous, healthy baby. But, as Fern's first winter approached, she developed a high fever. I'd just called Aunt Peg for her advice. I was surprised she called me back the same day.

"There is very sad news," she said. "Jon's brother hooked up his car's exhaust in his garage last night. He killed himself over regretting that he left his pregnant wife for his pregnant secretary. You must tell Jon when he gets home. Then Jon needs to call his mom. She is a mess."

"What do you mean she's a mess?" I asked, though I knew what Aunt Peg would say next.

"She is lapsing into her Valium and scotch pattern from when Jon's dad died," she said.

Jon's addictions made more sense now. Apparently, his proclivity for pot and booze had genetic roots, as is the usual. Jon's mother was just as nervous a woman as my mother, but she self-medicated with drugs and booze rather than food, as Mom did. This loss was enough to send her spiraling out of control again. Her second husband could no longer hold her habit in check.

I stayed home with recuperating baby Fern when Jon and Jessa made their sad pilgrimage east. Jon and his brother had never been close, but this event marked a downward spiral for Jon, now an only son with a needy bereaved mother.

***

In 1986, Jon rescued two draft horses and bought a neighbor's barn that he rebuilt in our back field. He spent a lot of time in that barn and a lot of money we did not have on these huge, older horses. At my insistence, he found another home for the horses. But Jon grew dour and drank more. Then he lost his job when taking a disabled adult out for a beer one night en route from work. Jon admitted it was a stupid thing to do but blamed his firing on his boss. At the time, I bought into her heartlessness, still in denial of Jon's problem. The only job prospects Jon now had in our rural county would be with the board of education as a teacher, where the need was greatest. Jon subbed for the school system, just as I did, while he enrolled in a master's program in early childhood education. Every college paper he turned in had been rewritten by me. The completion of my own master's degree was on hold, after taking only three night-school classes.

***

We were persevering through our relationship while enjoying our lovely girls. There was nothing we loved doing more than sitting them together in their play room with toys surrounding them, even though they often found an empty diaper box more thrilling.

Our ninth wedding anniversary was upon us. Surely on the night we resurrected our romance, pregnancy could not occur while breastfeeding and during that time of the month. Yet it did. With no insurance, we discovered right before Fern's first birthday party that I was pregnant. Dr. Paul confirmed it days later. Our dear doctor was kind enough to charge us minimally for the prenatal care he knew was required, including the amniocentesis procedure. Now having become pregnant so effortlessly, we assured Dr. Paul we would have him perform my tubal ligation as soon as this, our last baby, was born.

***

Our phone system was so rudimentary and rural, we were on a party line. This meant the three families on our mountain all had separate ring tones that rang in each other's homes. At Hazel's house, I could answer my calls if I heard my double ring. In the fall of 1986, while sitting in her home, we heard the peal of my ring. It was Dr. Paul's nurse calling with news.

"Are you sitting down? Great. The tests show you have an XY, a boy."

"But we don't do XYs—we only do girls!" I stammered, stunned, but overjoyed.

For Dad's sixty-second birthday, we gave him the news that he would have a grandson. Dad also received the news that I had been accepted into the MENSA organization. Dad had told me once that this was a club for people with high IQs and that I could *never* get in. My news proved him wrong and he was truly surprised and proud of this accomplishment.

Unlike my father, I refused to underestimate my own daughter's intellectual potential. She loved reading her flashcard words and singing nursery rhymes. I read to her every day on our mountaintop. Neighbor Sally, a Head Start teacher, was able to get Jessa into her program when asked because she was "geographically challenged." This designation confirmed we *really did* live far out in the boondocks.

Jessa loved school and tested early to qualify as a student in gifted education.

***

On a lovely April day, I delivered my third baby, again on the twenty-second day of the month. Ford arrived with his dad's stunning red hair, but unlike us, he had chestnut brown eyes. Surely this healthy son was the blessing we needed to seal our love and our family. The delivery was quick and virtually painless. Ford was baptized in our home by Reverend Bob, who had replaced our female minister. Will and his wife were among the friends present. I had recommitted to Jon and ended my affair with Will. Parenthood had turned us into more conservative thinkers now. Jon got a full-time job teaching early intervention classes to children with disabilities. Our calendar was full with friends' parties, night classes, and one very exciting theater event ahead for me.

Cliff and Jim were two extremely creative minds, as well as friends of ours. The first was a wood artist and theater director who had married one of my closest friends and Fern's godmother, Karin. The second was a drama teacher and pianist. They had directed me in past productions. They came to me with an offer—the role of Aldonza in *Man of La Mancha*. We had seen stage, television, and film actor Richard Kiley perform *Don Quixote* in Pittsburgh years before. Ford was just a baby, but with the help of babysitting friends, I became Aldonza, my forever-favorite role. Cliff played Quixote and Will played the comical role of the innkeeper.

Will asked me to perform for a benefit toward his purchase of an old church that he wanted to convert into a theater. It was an opportunity to promote the upcoming musical as well. I had not sung on stage for years, but I wore my peasant costume, knelt on the stage of a packed house, and sang my favorite song from the show. To calm my nerves, I directed my gaze upward and sang to one of the stained-glass windows on the side wall.

"When you sang 'Dulcinea' onstage," Will told me afterward, "I fell in love with you all over again. For the months we have been apart, it has felt as though I were truly dead inside.

On my deathbed, I swear to you I will have visions of you passing before my eyes," he literally cried.

Now, decades later, ever clear are Will's words, which lured me then back into his arms.

For a second theater benefit, I sang torch songs in a 1950's vintage evening gown, alongside a piano. I sang one song for Jon and another for Will, a few for both. I never lied to Jon when I saw Will. I couldn't bear the added guilt of lying that usually accompanies affairs.

This was the true definition of an open marriage, one which Jon had encouraged, and Will's wife had initiated years before. After all, Jon and I had made it to eleven years of marriage. We celebrated that date with our three small children. Jon set the camera's timer for what would end up being our last family photo. I wore my wedding gown and our children were in our arms before our hearth.

A month later Jon went away to an early intervention conference. He came home and was honest about an affair he had begun while there, with a woman named Eula Lee. He seemed glad to hear of my having been cast as Nancy, the lead in *Oliver*. Will played opposite me in the role of Bill Sykes. Now, instead of playing Jon's lover onstage, I would croon, "As Long as He Needs Me" to Will. I was too caught up in my delusion of our safely feathered nest to know we were playing with deadly fire.

***

Jon built a carport and bought an old Harley-Davidson motorcycle. He worked on it incessantly in his crude workshop, rather than spend time with the children and me. It was déjà vu to his days of going out back to tend to his old horses for hours. A motorcycle became the object of my jealousy, the symbol of the growing trouble in our marriage. I was not about to get on it, and I certainly did not want our children getting rides down the rutted dirt road. One spring day, my neighbor, and by now trusted friend Sally, called me on our shared party line.

"Take a walk in the woods below your home and take along a large garbage bag."

I followed her instructions and completely filled a bag with empty half-gallon bottles of Southern Comfort. Then it was out to the workshop to find a hidden barrel filled to the brim with cigarette butts. The reason I had failed to detect either was Jon smoked whiskey-flavored pipe tobacco. This hid the smell of both the cigarettes and whiskey. I'd been played, a fool in denial.

I called Sally to tell her of my find and begged her to be completely up front with me.

"When he gets home, look deep under the seat of his Jeep, and see what you will find."

I lined up all the found whiskey bottles on the massive oak picnic table he had built.

When the Jeep pulled up, I waited for his eyes to land on the unique picnic table display.

"Do you think you might have a teensy problem?" I asked, beginning the confrontation.

"I don't have a fucking problem," he snarled at me like a cornered, wild, rabid dog.

I ran over to the Jeep and pulled a half-empty whiskey bottle from under his driver's seat.

"Oh, I'd say you have a big one."

He ignored me and stomped into the house, glowering. I followed him and began recounting all he was risking… again. He drew his fist back and was ready to punch me in my face, but six little eyes were watching the scene unfold around us.

"How does it feel to hit your wife in front of your kids?" I snarled back at him.

At this, he crumpled to the floor in tears. We ended our marriage then. Jon would always put his alcohol and pot before his family. With deep sadness, I finally surrendered to this knowledge.

A month later he told me he was leaving us for his Eula Lee, who enjoyed riding his motorcycle and smoking pot with him. I begged him to consider counseling, moving, praying, anything for the sake of our kids. As he walked with me outside, away from the children's ears, I unexpectedly spotted a tattoo under his tee shirt sleeve—another moment frozen in my memory. I lifted the short sleeve and was stunned at what I saw.

"Damn, it *must* be love to permanently put Eula Lee's name in a heart on your arm!"

The next day, I mailed every romantic card my husband had ever given me to the other woman's office, showing her what their affair was ending. I was smart enough to convince Jon to travel to the courthouse and sign over the deed to the home, which my grandmother's hard-earned money had allowed us to purchase. I was savvy enough to hire a divorce attorney before he left us. I was sane enough to write this journal entry:

"My love for him is crumbling daily with very little hope. The children, ages two, three, and six, are too young to realize the real changes this will bring about. It will be for the best. Jon has been so very abusive as a closet alcoholic. Even Will called him to try and talk sense into him. Jessa tells me she is not upset or scared, rather relieved he is leaving us in peace. How will this affect her, years from now? I'm not naïve enough to think that it won't."

Jessa made a list of Daddy's behaviors and the things we'd no longer have to deal with, in an effort to comfort us. She wrote, "Say bad words, drink and drive, smoke around us, hit or kick us, break things, do things for us, take us places as a family, give us any money, make us have to move."

Reading her list, I ached for the children's lost ideal of a good, healthy, reliable father more than my own loss of a husband.

***

In late June 1989, Jon piled his possessions into the bed of his red beater truck and left us on a rutted road in the middle of hillbilly heaven. The four of us stood atop our mountain by our chalet log home, watching as he pulled away. That moment is frozen in my mind like the scene before intermission in *Gone with the Wind*. Tomorrow was another day. The children did not realize the full impact of what was happening. He would marry Eula Lee, who would leave him with huge debts in less than three years. Jessa's list underscored to me how very pathetic he was. In a short time, my seething anger transformed into pure pity for him and real relief for the four of us. I was so much stronger and determined to better my children's lives. The first step would be initializing a plan to get off of that muddy mountain in the middle of nowhere.

In the remaining few months atop the mountain, I took the time to watch and reflect on my beautiful children. Their father had model good-looks, thus they were blessed with both of our best features. But what was missing other than his positive physical attributes? My next mate would have to be a man with a much higher intellect. Jon's desire to be buzzed or high every day did not show someone with deep thought or ambition. I would never again live in the middle of a rural, poverty-stricken county with a boring man who had no desires greater than to watch reruns, drink beer, and tinker with motorcycle engines. My children deserved a better education and far better opportunities in a healthy environment. And they deserved to have a better, healthier father.

CHAPTER FIVE
New Ballpark

My old friend Liz, whom I had met investigating an insurance claim, gave me useful advice: "Cry for three days, say 'excess baggage,' and move on." The excess baggage was all the abuse we had suffered due to Jon's addictions and outbursts. My pal told me to visualize dumping the bag by the roadside. I did so by immersing myself in directing Tennessee Williams's *The Rose Tattoo* in Will's theater. This classic comedy about Italian immigrants in Florida, centering around a middle-aged love affair, is rarely performed. Children play together in the opening scene. Will's two moppets and Jessa brought this scene to life. Will was cast as the priest, and his wife performed the role of the Strega, or the Italian witch. All performances opened to a full house. Directing was as much, if not more, fun than acting.

***

Liz and I made plans to rent an old Victorian manor in a quaint village…until Dad found it full of asbestos. Liz visited me often, now divorced and in love with another Mr. Wrong who delivered appliances. But she was free and fun and feisty and I needed her energy and sister-love. On weekends, we would hire a sitter and go out dancing in a club on the outskirts of the nearest small town. We protected each other from lechers when necessary. Her friendship, along with my adorable children, carried me through Jon's abandonment.

In August, Fern and her friends celebrated her fourth birthday at McDonald's. She was a sweet light of joy in my life, a little joker attached to "her baby," Ford, whom she played mama to.

My curious parents called Jon's mother, who immediately blamed my affair with Will for Jon's desertion. Despite his alcoholism and abuse, they found me fully at fault. My phone rang.

"We have never sinned as bad as you have. We do not approve of your lifestyle," my mother said, which I understood to mean she was talking about being divorced. Then just before she hung up, she added, "I have been ill with nerves over this," sealing her stinging betrayal. And that was the entire conversation.

Where was their support while I continued working toward my master's degree at night? Conversely, Aunt Peg, who was contemplating if she should divorce, was supportive and kind. In time, though, even my mother-in-law, hoping the marriage could be saved, and warming to my situation, said she understood my bitterness at her son's leaving us for his lover. In the fall of '89, after eleven years of marriage, our divorce was final. That same day, I accepted a position as a caseworker for severely emotionally disturbed teens in foster care. We would have to move off the muddy mountain. It was impossible anyway to stay during winter in our log home. Splitting logs for the woodstove proved impossible, and my Schatzie had recently scared away a brown bear attempting to scratch through our window screens. My loyal Doberman was now our proven protector. We found renters for my home, along with a used station wagon to purchase. I signed a lease on a split-level home in a small college town. I became the model of enthusiasm for our new life to my young children.

***

Three days after the divorce, I unintentionally kept Jon waiting when he came to pick up the kids. Before us all stood a grubby, angry man reeking of booze. In front of our children he said, "I wish you would die!" He was angry over the $550 child support he was court-ordered to pay monthly. My divorce attorney had explained that the amount had been fairly and formulaically computed based upon our salaries.

***

I am sure Jon was also angry about leaving the home of *his* dreams. Though I'd found renters to live there, they would not be clean or respectful of my property over the next few years. The home had deteriorated just as our marriage had. The ever-wet basement now had a wide variety of fungi living there. The wood on the mudroom floor had long ago given way underfoot, as termites had infested our foundation…a costly lesson. A long black snake had been found wrapped around the inside of the mudroom window one day. Carpenter bees had bored holes through many of the logs. The windows were so drafty that plastic had to be attached with a blow dryer every fall through spring.

One side of the wrap-around deck had rotted and was torn down. In short, it had never been the home of my dreams, and I spent the next few years praying specifically, "Lord help me to sell that house on the mountain. Find some fool somewhere."

***

I paid a neighbor to drive a thirty-foot truck with our belongings for our move eighty miles away. Our cat, Liebes, adjusted nicely to a warmer house, taking his usual spot at the bottom of Jessa's bed. Schatzie first moved with Jon to his meager rental on the other side of the county, until Jessa reported, "Daddy hit her hard with a jug, in front of us!"

"Don't spy on my life!" Jon had yelled, making Jessa cry, but not denying her accusation.

Our dog came to live with us in a fenced-in lot, her days to run in pristine fields over.

***

Will was obsessed with seeing me whenever he could. My last hours in my log chalet were with him. After the move, he drove in the mid-winter to see me, proclaiming his love for me. He could not end his broken marriage then, though he would in due time. The longing I felt for Will was intense. There was a palpable ache in my chest when I imagined him, every day, for months.

There is no question that I was in love with this Aries artist. He was a creative, tender lover, but what made him unique was the way he verbalized his love for me. We were in relationships so lacking in passion and true commitment that we were starved for one another's adoring words.

He wrote this letter to me on New Year's Day and mailed it with his tear splotches all over the pages:

It hurts me not to go to you, but I cannot. It is time for you to find someone who can accept the gift of your beautiful love, fully and completely. Please do this. Find a good man to love you and your children. Try to understand how difficult it is for me. I love you and will always.

Love, Will

Bereft, my immediate answer was:

I am sure that my partner for the second half of my life will come in time. But the time is not now and seeing you a few times a year will not interfere until he makes his appearance on a white steed. I am eighty miles away, always open to your strong arms, your beautiful deep kisses, and your every need.

I am absolutely your soul mate, Leigh

Will was resolute in ending the relationship. He knew he was standing in the way of my future and that of my children. The guilt of contributing to the ending of my marriage ate him up.

Just when we were getting used to our newfound home, it was sold in the spring, so we moved to a house just across the street. The blue house needed much tender loving care, so I painted, decorated, cleaned, and curtained it in exchange for a minimal rent. It was small but had more character and charm that our previous rental. But, once the new nest was feathered, I realized how lonely I was for adult friendship.

"There are no friendly women in this snooty college town," I whined to a new guy friend.

This helpful local photographer picked up the phone in my living room. "Maggie, I am inviting my new friend to your group. What night and what time shall I tell her to be there?"

There, I met Maggie, a teacher with two children who was going through her own divorce. We became best friends for many years, and we supported each other through our single-mom period. Liz was my first friend to divorce due to abuse, but here was a friend in my new neighborhood who simply fell out of love with her mate. She shared with me that a teacher of her daughter had referred to our children as "victims of divorce." Maggie volleyed back that if children were victims, then they may soon be in a majority, with a growing number of divorces.

I had gone from one who could not imagine divorce, to a divorcée with divorced friends.

***

In 1990, our newly fatherless family took a much-needed East Coast vacation. We visited my college friend Joy, with whom we celebrated Fern's fifth birthday. In her large country estate near the Jersey shore, Vernon made the short drive to meet my children. He and Joy's college lover were still friends, as were Joy and I. He had begged me to come back to him, but our time together was long over. On an impulse, I put the tip of his finger in my mouth, saying to my children, "Mm, tastes like chocolate!" The children found it hilarious. It was soothing to hear his lovely deep bass laugh again. Thankfully, my kids had never been exposed to bigotry. They were at ease with this striking man who obviously adored their mother. Thereafter, Vernon would call me each year to wish me a happy birthday...and to see if he could change my mind.

***

From Joy's home, we visited the Jersey shore, where a sudden wave sent three-year-old Ford crashing down, sopping wet. My tears of sadness fell into the sea's edge as I lifted him, smelled the pure baby scent of his copper hair mixed with sea salt. Jon was missing his beautiful son staring in wonderment at the ocean for the first time. Ford would not even remember his father. Jon was missing two beautiful little daughters giggling as they chased each other on the beach, casting shadows as they blocked the setting sun. I wore my happy face for my children most of the time, but these images crushed me as I faced the enormity of the sea and the gargantuan task ahead of my single mother status to three young children.

***

Though my job was interesting, less than a year into it, I soon found another with higher pay as a supervisor and therapist at a home for juvenile delinquents. This new position arose when Fern started kindergarten, so at least my largest expense of Montessori school tuition was now halved. Fern and Jessa were bright, eager students. Ford was a comical imp at preschool who "played nicely with the other children." His teachers frequently commented on his high social intelligence. He exuded charm, even as a preschooler.

Around this same time, Jon sent me a letter saying he was going to "enjoy life and stop paying support." He moved far to the south and rarely came to see the kids. Then, out of the blue that fall, he showed up in a beater van to take them camping. I spotted a case of beer hidden in the backseat and turned back into Mama Grizzly, fearing my cubs were in danger. At my request, Maggie literally kept me from attacking him when she came by to mediate. He did take them for one night during which time I prayed incessantly for their safety. I had zero trust in him by now.

***

Following this, Jon made a bogus abuse report to Child Protective Services because Fern peed in his car, for fear of asking him to stop at a bathroom. Somehow this was a reflection on my mothering. In response to this ruse, I told him, "If you take my kids from me, I will surely kill you." Did he really want to take them when he wouldn't even pay for their support?

***

At the start of 1991, a divorced engineer with two daughters entered my life through a mutual friend. He was kind, smart, and he wanted to marry me. Yet in my core I felt no passion. My honesty broke his heart. As good a life as he wanted to give me, Will had set the passion precedent, and I could not settle for less. He had insisted that we each meet one another's parents, as they did not live very far apart. He too was an only child. I ended the relationship after six months, disappointing my mother once again.

"You should have snatched him up," Mom declared. "What man will want you with Jessa, Fern, and Ford?"

With her intonation, she might as well have said, "With syphilis, gonorrhea, and chlamydia?"

***

Nana Marie now lived with my parents in their home. Always depressed and very frail, she visited me for a few days. While I assisted with bathing her, she told me Mom never once offered to do the same. How sad. How I had missed her! The drive to my parents was just around two hours away, and yet my life was consumed with raising my children and working full-time. But she understood; she'd been divorced, though she had waited until my mother was grown.

To add to my load, the job at the boys' home became unbearable due to my atheist boss.

"It was brought to my attention you actually recommended prayer to a client," she said.

What I told her was that I had simply been explaining the importance of a bedtime routine by stating the routine of my three-year-old: put on pajamas, brush teeth, wash face, say prayers, turn the lights out. Why did I even have to defend what I had done? This juvenile delinquent was fighting his lights-out rule.

"What you did was to impose your values on a client!" she barked from her sour face.

"Is prayer a *bad* suggestion as a part of a bedtime routine?" I responded.

"Yes, it certainly is, and I do not want to hear of it again!" she said with vitriol.

Case closed. I wanted far away from her.

I found a similar job in a southern city as a crisis counselor. The kids and I made several unsuccessful trips to find housing. We did not like the look of the area. It was far away and bleak. At the same time, an interview came along for a fascinating job as a professional advocate for the mandated protection and advocacy agency for the disabled. My office would be out of my home. I admired my interviewer, Fran, for her quiet strength, which she used to fight for the rights of her clients. This was finally a job I would relish, seeking justice for the disabled.

As we were packing up boxes to move for the first job offering, the phone rang. Fran was on the line, offering me this second job.

"Jessa, Fern, Ford, come here," I said, as soon as I'd hung up the phone. "Do you want to help Mommy unpack the boxes and stay here…or do you want to move south?"

"Stay here!" they all said in unison, with grins plastered on their sweet faces.

This unique and rewarding job was tailored to my personality. My passion for defending underdogs from bullies would take on new meaning for the next six years. Suddenly, I felt taller, younger, and stronger, like new purpose had been shot through my veins.

CHAPTER SIX
Pitcher Change

Weeks after becoming an advocate, Maggie invited me to a Labor Day picnic where her ex brought a friend. He was a tall, heavy-set, balding-but-boyish Luciano Pavarotti look-alike. Or maybe more Bluto from *Popeye*.

He introduced himself as Wolf, telling me that he was the new lawyer in town. And then he cut to the chase. "Wanna go out sometime?" he asked.

"Oh, honey," I remember answering right back, "I do not date men more than ten years my junior, but thanks for asking."

"Your birthday?" he asked, and we produced our driver's licenses. The difference in age was short one month of ten years.

"Looks like I just made the cut. Where do you want to go out on a date, *honey?*"

We both laughed, and our relationship was born.

I have always been intrigued by wolves, being the forerunner of dogs, so even his name, shortened from Wolfgang, drew me in. If Jon fell for me quickly, it seemed

Wolf fell faster, and he courted me aggressively. He was the first man I was attracted to in two years of dating too many losers and users. I had rightfully been choosy, wanting a man who was the polar opposite of Jon. Wolf was a man with a doctorate and ambition, and a man who, years later, said during a marriage counseling session that I was "all he was looking for in a woman and more." He *needed* my love. This need to be needed in order to fix someone, as I later learned, is the first step in a co-dependent relationship.

***

Wolf enjoyed the finer things in life. Yet, his childhood was spartan growing up in the next county north. He pursued me by taking me out to fancy dinners and ordering the most expensive items. He showed me off at social events with other big fish in the minuscule bowl of what was his small college town. His baby face topped a huge man's body that could lift me easily into the air. He traced my nose with his finger, announcing its perfection. He definitely fell hard for me first.

Wolf had been the victim of abusive step-parenting, so he assured me he would do right by my three. Forget what psych classes had taught me about parental modeling. I believed him. He first met Ford when his sisters had dressed their toddler brother up in a tutu for their amusement.

"This boy needs a dad!" he bemoaned, shaking his head.

"No, all three children need one," I told him. *Was he truly up to it?* I wondered.

***

In the fall of 1991, Nana was diagnosed with colon cancer. The colostomy only prolonged the inevitable. When we visited her at a second-rate private care home, the engagement ring of Wolf's deceased mother was on my finger, though we weren't *formally* engaged. He wanted me to know that he loved me and therefore entrusted me with his only material reminder of his long-deceased mother. Seeing the ring and seeing the children brought a feeble smile to my nana's pained face. That same night, Jon called me.

"How've you been?" he said, and I felt as though a bolt of lightning came out of nowhere.

"Great," I said. I took a deep breath and then put it all out right there on the table. "I'll be marrying a lawyer in a few months."

"Okay. I'll be visiting soon," he said, and then promptly hung up. He never visited again.

***

Aunt Peg told me years later the purpose of Jon's call that day was to ask me to consider reconciling. He was stunned to learn our lives were moving on without him. Even without Wolf, my answer would have been not only no, but *hell* no! My heart was now set on this young lawyer.

Wolf was employed by the largest law firm in town. All attorneys in the firm, which provided counselors for the local hospital, were expected to attend the hospital charity benefit ball. By the time we went, we were smitten with each other. I could not wait to show Nana our "prom photo," but at her bedside, days after Christmas, she was too weak to focus on it. She died days into the new year. My biggest supporter and nurturer resided in Heaven now, holding her perfectly beautiful great-granddaughter. No one had ever loved me from the depths of her heart like she had. From the realm of Heaven, if Nana could bless my children in some way, I believed she would surely do it. Wolf understood my grief, as his grandfather had raised him and supported him through law school. In fact, his grandfather had been just as generous as was my nana. He gifted us with a large down payment for our new home. This gift signaled Grandpa's approval of our union.

***

In 1992, we began looking for our future home. Wolf made the decision to leave the firm and begin his private practice with one employee, a tireless, underpaid secretary. Wolf was idealistic in his desire to help clients, yet he was often stung financially by those who convinced him they had done nothing wrong when they were guilty as sin. And he did not like his fellow lawyers or the little white lies they developed on behalf of their clients. He certainly did not take losing well in the courtroom. He would stew for days following an unexpected guilty verdict on behalf of his clients.

Most importantly, he was ill-prepared for the stresses of owning his own business. He began drinking in bars and schmoozing up to attorneys and potential clients. With me, he relaxed by house hunting and attending auctions. We bought our home in the same village where Liz and I had coveted a home years before. Built in 1890 by a doctor, the Victorian mansion had sixteen rooms, a wrap-around porch, a turret, and an expansive backyard.

The sellers were in a financial bind, so it didn't take long to negotiate the sale. It was our dream home, the grandest in the village, and it would be the site of our wedding. We furnished, decorated, gardened, painted, and planned. A large garden was plowed in the back yard. He insisted Jessa would help him plant and weed it. She detested this new responsibility.

We now lived in an economically depressed village. My children's classmates stood with their mouths agape when visiting. At Halloween, trick-or-treaters entered into an ornate oak parlor with a grand staircase with original stained-glass light fixtures. Wolf told an Oliver Twist look-alike to dig into the candy bowl with both hands. Ford told me this child in his kindergarten class was from a poor family. Even my kindergartner could see how differently we lived now.

Jessa made a best friend, Tanya, from the neighboring trailer court. Her dad had recently passed away from cancer. Wolf developed a deep dislike for Tanya, who would shut down when he was around. Clearly, she was afraid of him. Wolf claimed she was sneaky, when in fact she was merely shy near his huge, glaring presence.

***

Wolf's grandpa moved in with us before Christmas of 1992. We converted a room off the first-floor parlor into his bedroom, where he chose to sleep in his recliner. Wolf's father and sister visited, both angry at Grandpa's acceptance of our invitation. Their anger began when they learned of Grandpa's monetary gift toward our home, now his home also. Medicare-provided home health nurses visited regularly to bathe and monitor him, so it was no strain on us. This gentle, frail man was a pleasure to have in our home, and he was a welcoming calming influence on Wolf.

An early spring snowstorm brought deep drifts and harsh winds. Schatzie lived in a doghouse outside at this point due to her incontinence. During the storm, she wandered off to the blue Appalachian hills behind our home to die in peace. She knew her job as nanny had been performed with grace. She saved me the grief of watching her death. My connection to this dog remains in my heart forever, the protector of my babies on our muddy mountain. "God will prepare everything for our perfect happiness in Heaven, and if it takes my dog being there, I believe he'll be there," said Dr. Billy Graham, when asked to speak on the subject in his syndicated column of March 14, 2011. So I believe it's not a "maybe" or a "what if" then that I will joyously greet my sweet Schatzie in Heaven, along with all of my other beloved pets.

Grandpa died three days before our wedding. He told us before his death to go forward with our wedding as planned. What an honor it was, I felt, to be present at his death with Wolf. "Go with Jesus. Go to your wife and daughter there," I said as he took his last deep breath. He crossed over beautifully.

***

Our marriage took place in the spring of '93 on Aunt Peg's birthday, though she was too frail to attend. My friends catered the event as their wedding gift. My country neighbor Sally and Jessa played a flute duet. My three children were my bridal attendants. Wolf's senile great uncle officiated. He called me "Ingrid" throughout the ceremony. The reception was a grand party inside our restored Victorian mansion. My parents smiled from ear to ear. It seemed that my folks were finally pleased with a decision of mine.

My husband was an educated, seemingly wealthy, WASP-y guy…their dream son-in-law with a showplace home. I had done something right for once, or at least I hoped so. I had just turned thirty-eight and married my second husband, with our lavish home as the setting. It seemed like a vast improvement over the last husband and the last house. But was it?

CHAPTER SEVEN
Rule Change

We spent our honeymoon in Cozumel, which was overly commercialized, full of "Hey Joes," and oppressively hot. Our next vacation that year would take us to Bar Harbor, where we stayed at a different bed and breakfast each night. My parents babysat on these getaways. They were doting grandparents, and I appreciated their support through this second time at bat.

It didn't take long, though, for things to start feeling off in our marriage. Wolf let me know up front about my "free rent." He did not seem to understand the concept that wives did not pay rent. He insisted we keep our financial accounts separate. My responsibilities were to pay for food and utilities for his enormous house of over six thousand square feet. I told him this notion was cheap and strange, but he would not budge. Renting movies that *he* wanted to watch on weekends was his grandiose treat, and, in his snarky way, he reminded us of this treat often.

***

My job consisted of interventions and mediations on behalf of disabled children or deinstitutionalized adults when rights violations were suspected. The northern third of our rural state was my territory. I traveled mountain roads in bad weather in an old car, with no cell phone.

Class-action lawsuits were enforced in an effort to deinstitutionalize people with disabilities. One of my assignments was working with the families of those same poor souls who I had seen on the ward in my graduate school night class years ago. My job was to answer the family's concerns over their loved one's transition into a group home. My other duty was to monitor those homes for any rights violations—and they happened: abuse, staff shortages, theft, even death. Just as with insurance claims, client cases were referred to me from a central office.

My most memorable case involved several poor families who lived in a rural county and whose children attended a relatively poor school system. These families had bonded over their disabled children being mistreated by an inept teacher. This teacher did not follow the students individualized plans and utilized her own unauthorized punishments instead of positive reinforcement. She used duct tape to restrain children, my clients, in a time-out chair and once even left a child, also my client, sitting in her own vomit to "teach her a lesson."

I worked with the families, the director of special education, the superintendent, and our attorney toward the goal of transferring that teacher out of special education. This meant going to every child's team meeting for more than three months after meeting individually with many families in their homes. Near Christmastime, we received word that our efforts had paid off and a new teacher was in the classroom. After our final morning meeting, I was ceremoniously escorted back to a "double-wide in the holler," as they called it. There, the families surprised me with a potluck dinner and two simple gifts. They had fashioned a Christmas angel out of handkerchiefs and made a hand-written plaque for me, thanking me for being their angel on behalf of their kids. The best part was that my services cost them nothing. I still treasure that hand-crafted angel, now stained with ages of many Christmases.

Traveling country roads in wintertime to help my clients across the state, I soon needed a new car. Wolf's cousin, who owned a bank in a nearby town, did me a favor. He sold me a bank-repossessed Subaru at a bargain price and gave me some wise investment advice. My log home finally sold—an answered prayer. Wolf had the expertise to close the deal without Realtors. A wealthy young widow nabbed it up at a bargain price. Wolf slyly told me to put the closing check into *his* account for safekeeping, officially co-mingling our marital assets. This was another example of his shady behavior toward my money, yet he earned so much more than I!

In 1995, I finally had more time for my family with the completion of my master's in counseling. It had taken me six years of night classes to earn that degree. My employer did not increase my salary for this achievement, though excellent medical benefits for my husband and children were provided. We would soon be accessing them.

During Fern's dental checkup, X-rays revealed the stunted development of her permanent teeth. The dentist recommended a blood test. The results of that test showed her liver enzymes and cholesterol were elevated to the point where she should have been in a coma. An endocrinologist gave us the bad news—her thyroid gland was likely not functioning at all, and there was a possibility of thyroid cancer.

Then we heard the good news—she had Hashimoto's disease and a daily dose of Synthroid would spur her on to normal growth. I thought she simply had my Irish grandma's short genes, though Ford was a whole head taller. Fern was placed into remedial classes in math and reading. Her academic tests showed difficulties in learning comprehension and staying on task. Being in the business of dealing with special education, I requested a psychological workup, and we learned Fern had a learning disability called auditory processing deficit. She would have to work hard to keep her grades up but could succeed with an individual educational plan tailored to her needs, such as being away from distractions and having study guides. Her mama was now *her* professional advocate and at least her lawyer stepfather attended her school meetings twice a year. Working beside strong mothers when advocating for countless children throughout the state had taught me quite well.

A very troubling sign of Wolf's dysfunction occurred when Fern had her tenth birthday party. She invited Tanya as one of her guests, as she had been like a second older sister to Fern. When Wolf saw Jessa's best friend present, he screamed, "Why is she here? It's sickening that this party can't be about Fern and her friends."

He was rude, loud, and intimidating to all the girls, effectively ruining the party.

"Fern invited Tanya," I defended, trying my utmost to veil my disgust at his outburst.

He glared at Jessa, and she, of course, cried. Tanya was even more scared of him now. This pattern of bullying directed at Jessa would increase…yet she was a model daughter.

I also became increasingly disappointed with Wolf's broken promise to father Ford through sports. He bragged about his mastery of basketball in high school, yet the imparting of these skills down to Ford never actualized. Wolf was always at his office and seemed to actually have no clue how to interact with children. Ford played sports on neighborhood teams coached by his friends' fathers. My abilities in team sports were nil. Since he didn't have much athletic guidance from home, Ford learned instead to use his sense of humor and God-given charm to endear to others. That high social intelligence of his proved to be a gift and has served him well in attaining his life goals.

At least Wolf shared my love of dogs, so we studied breeds and chose a Rhodesian Ridgeback, once famed for its bravery in guarding against lion attacks. Tasha was a golden beauty. Stubborn, she went through training class twice, yet grew to be an easy-going family pet.

Liebes, my loyal cat who had been with me since my first days with Jon, went into seizures one afternoon. I asked Wolf to meet me at the vet's office and he quickly obliged. The cat's liver was failing. Euthanizing Liebes was the compassionate end for our sweet gray tabby of eighteen years. He died peacefully in my arms. Wolf dug his grave and buried him in our backyard.

We took the kids on a vacation to Disney World to ease the pain of losing their pet. As most parents do, we went on all the rides we could before collapsing in exhaustion. On our way home, we visited my ex-in-laws for the last time. Several times before, we had gone out of our way to see them, yet they never reciprocated. Their cold awkwardness made more sense when I later learned they had cut their grandchildren out of their lives and their will. The loss was theirs. Still, I had a hard time with their decision. The abandonment of their father was hard enough on my kids' psyches, but by their paternal grandparents purposely rejecting them, it was a double whammy. The door had been open on my end for their continued involvement in the lives of the children. As my own grandparents were such powerful nurturers in my life, it just made no sense to me that grandparents could turn away from their own grandchildren.

When we returned from our trip, we learned that my father had to undergo a quadruple bypass. With wild arrhythmia, his heart barely survived the operation. The cardiologist warned him to begin a lifestyle of healthy diet and exercise, or he would be back in twenty years for the same operation. The latter would prove to be true. At least my children had doting maternal grandparents, who were proving to be kinder and more generous than they were as parents.

CHAPTER EIGHT
Strike Two

Just as I had been promoted in the insurance business to work alongside a lawyer, my job as an advocate often involved developing high-profile lawsuits on behalf of clients for litigation by our firm's contracted attorney. Ian was an Irish charmer, à la Spencer Tracy. He was divorced, and he became my work friend. He met Wolf, and they instantly disliked each other. Wolf was jealous of more successful attorneys, particularly an unmarried one who spent so much time with his wife going to meetings and trainings statewide. But I had learned my lesson in fidelity. Though Ian tried valiantly to seduce me, my faithfulness prevailed despite increasing marital problems. It became apparent that Wolf was jealous of other men to the point of craziness.

For example, Wolf hired prisoners he defended to work on our house projects. While the workers were there, Wolf called me in the middle of my workday in my office at home.

"Just what are you doing now?" he barked over the phone, breathing heavily.

"Oh, sunbathing topless on our upstairs porch," I sassed dryly to my maniac husband.

"That was a sick thing to say!" he screamed, after racing from his office to check on me.

Obviously, his need to get reduced labor trumped my safety with felons buzzing around.

Wolf knew of my history with Jon, yet he came home drunk too often. When he parked in the middle of our backyard instead of in our driveway, we fought. The result was a signed paper saying he would quit boozing. The next time he came home drunk, he went to thirteen-year-old Jessa's room in his tighty-whities crying for her to mediate between us. She was disgusted at the sight of this barely clothed, obese, balding drunk.

"Mom, I wish he would die," she cried to me afterward.

A light bulb flashed brightly in my brain. But the light bulb burned hotter when he began to force sex on me as I wept. My prayer was for a door to open up. But I had to be the one to open that door by finding a job far away from him.

As our marriage unraveled, I learned the messy truths of his childhood, piece by piece. Wolf, like Jon, had an alcoholic mother. She lost her parental rights after she threw baby Wolf against a wall, breaking his arm, when she was drunk. His grandfather begged Child Protective Services not to take the baby, saying he would raise the child. Wolf's parents predictably divorced afterward. His mom ended up as yet another statistical DUI death. Wolf's dad remarried an abusive woman whose son by Wolf's dad would always be superior to her stepson.

Though he initially downplayed all this trauma, Wolf was emotionally damaged from the early abuse he suffered at home. Whenever he had the means to self-medicate with high-priced scotch, the cycle repeated itself. These closet skeletons never appeared during the courting process, but now, three years into the marriage, they hovered around us menacingly.

My kids had suffered enough. I arranged for the four of us to live with Maggie, my friend made through the photographer, in the summer of '96. I paid half her mortgage payment and our joint food bills. I went from sleeping in a grand Victorian home to tossing and turning on an air mattress in Maggie's front room. It was not about my comfort, though; rather it was about protecting my children, who had a peaceful summer in a brief respite from a building storm.

Jessa was friends with Maggie's daughter, and it was easy to have my work phone line transferred to Maggie's home and to work from there. How refreshing to live in a steady state of calm. There are times when another woman's presence is balm for the soul. Was this what it was like to share with a sister? And what could Wolf do about this, but acknowledge his faults to me and improve his behavior?

Aunt Peg called me that summer to tell me the latest bad news about my ex.

"He has really done it this time. He killed his girlfriend on his motorcycle due to his drunkenness," she said.

"Don't you mean his wife?" I asked.

"No, though he has a wife. This was a girlfriend," she said. "His mother says he is going from the hospital to the jail, but he may never walk again with crushing injuries to his upper legs."

"Were they wearing helmets?" I asked, though the answer to me was obvious.

"No, South Carolina says you don't have to…the state's way to cull the herd of idiots, I guess. He told the social worker in the hospital that he has no dependents," she informed me.

"Guess it's time to contact the hospital to set the social worker straight," I said. And that is just what I did.

Thereafter the children received small social security payouts during the time their father was deemed disabled. At that time, I also decided to pursue the delinquent child support he owed me, when I realized he had no intention of paying his debt. A school superintendent had dubbed me "a German shepherd who will not let go of a bone," in reference to my tenacity as a professional advocate. I drew strength from these words now, thinking, *Just wait. Grrr.*

***

At summer's end, Wolf came over to Maggie's house, sniveling and in a repentant mood, prompting my return to him. School was starting. The kids didn't need to change schools yet again. One divorce was hard enough. Shouldn't I give him one last try and persevere through these travails?

***

And it was an impressionable time for Jessa, who was beginning high school as first chair flute in band and had a sweet first love, JB. He was obviously smitten with her and also had the same large, shy eyes as Jessa. She hadn't felt such happiness in a long while, and she deserved it.

***

Then, the news came of Aunt Peg's death in the fall of 1996. She had suffered a stroke in her home. One of her nieces called me. I should have known it was coming. It must have been why she sent me a box of her most precious possessions: a diamond watch, a charm bracelet, an Egyptian scarab brooch, music boxes, figurines, antique dolls, scrimshaw, her tiny glass pelicans, and her framed needlepoint work. Aunt Peg had not wanted these sentimental items to be counted in her estate. She wanted them to be mine. This was her final way of telling me she loved me.

Fern and I drove to her funeral on the beautiful eastern shore of Maryland. My ex-mother-in-law and sister-in-law, Jessa's godmother, spoke as little as possible to us at the service, as though we were pariahs. But it was a treat to see some of Aunt Peg's best friends from working at the store decades earlier. They knew how special our connection was when they saw her watch and bracelet on my wrist. A guttural sob emerged from deep within me when we left the chapel with her ashes at the altar. My love for her was so great that I married into her family to connect her to my children. I was the daughter she never had, and she was my incredibly strong and non-judgmental mother figure.

Fern's loving companionship eased my deep grief on our return home. Aunt Peg was such a source of loving strength in my life. How could she be gone? Consolation came from envisioning this loving lady in Heaven holding my beautiful, healed baby…another who would reach across the divide to bless her great nieces and nephew. I would need her blessings.

***

Just because we returned to Wolf's mansion did not mean my job hunting ceased. First, there was a job offer in Annapolis as a social-work supervisor, but housing was scarce unless I crossed the often-jammed Bay Bridge twice a day. Being far away from friends and parents with no back-ups frightened me; thus, I declined the position. It was fortuitous that I kept my search going, as Wolf did not alter his drinking or his temper as promised. When he choked me against a third-floor banister in front of the children, I called the police.

I obtained a temporary restraining order against him. This gave me enough time to outline a plan to sell the antiques I had purchased for our house on my separate account. When Wolf learned of this, he was furious. He begged me to sell them to him so that they would remain in *his* house. He wrote me a fat check and I gladly accepted. He seemed more concerned with losing his furnishings than with losing his wife and stepchildren. He was most afraid of losing face as a big fish in his pathetic little pond. He warned me that no man would ever satisfy me the way he did. Oh, did he think highly of himself! He also told me that if I ever married another man, years later, when we thought he had long forgotten, he would hire one of his defendant thugs to find my new husband and smash his knee caps with a crowbar, leaving him in a ditch to never walk again. What a guy! Whatever love I had for him had turned to scorn. He was just more excess baggage.

The valuable lesson I learned was that even highly educated and ambitious men could succumb to addiction. Higher brain development did not defend against this scourge of mankind.

Without the drunken binges, which led to the temper outbursts, perhaps the marriage could have been saved. Wolf loved me and was willing to provide a better life for my children than they had had in the boonies. He valued education, hard work, and faith in God. But he was destined to resort to booze to numb a childhood of abuse by a stepparent. I would not allow the cycle of abuse to continue. Surely, somewhere out there was a better environment and a better father for my children. The door that I had been praying for was about to open wide.

I accepted a position with an advocacy nonprofit organization as executive director, and we moved out on the first day of 1997. Who's afraid of a big, bad Wolf? Not this little Red Riding Hood. We were about to celebrate an exciting move to a city with an image of strength, far away from the wolf. We would make our new home in the "Steel City," the city called Pittsburgh.

CHAPTER NINE
Fly Ball

My new job entailed traveling to offices in five small cities scattered across Pennsylvania. My main office could be located anywhere state-wide; thus, I chose to live in one of the state's top-rated school-systems. It was in a southern section of Pittsburgh. No one goes into the field of social services to make big money. And my BA in Psychology had been worthless. It prepared me for nothing specific in the job world. Now, even with my graduate degree, I knew that I would not earn a large salary. But I felt like a professional administrator for the first time, trying to help those who help folks less fortunate than myself. I could not fix the injustices within my first two marriages, but I could help make the region where we lived a better place for disabled clients.

My bosses were board members led by a charming executive named Ben. "We will not allow you to fail in this job," he assured me during our first meeting.

Board meetings took place in the state's center. My primary duty was to court voting members of the governor-appointed disability council, convincing them to funnel monies for nonprofits our way. The goal of our organization was promoting lifelong partnerships between adult role models and our clients, who were often lonely and poor. It was similar to Big Brothers/Big Sisters of America, with a warm and fuzzy ideology involving life-long time commitments.

As an adept saleswoman with an expense account, it was my pleasure to take our caring voters out to dinner. I found a rental home and an office space within a block of each other in the bustling suburb, where the pristine sidewalks led me from home to work each day.

To sell my organization effectively, I had to look sharp despite the prohibitive prices in the local trendy hair salons.

"Where do normal people on normal salaries get their hair done?" I asked a neighbor.

"I'll give you Jill's number. She works out of her home. You will love her," she said.

I kept Jill busy with regular appointments at her reasonable prices. She was easy to talk to, unlike my fourteen-year-old. Jessa had become downright sullen, she was so angry with me. She delayed her move to Pittsburgh, choosing to stay with Wolf for three weeks to complete her first semester at her first high school. It made sense for her to finish out the semester. I agreed to her staying as a peace offering because she had been so angry that she did not speak to me. She missed her first love, JB, and she missed life in a small village. Just before she moved, Wolf went from being abusive to coddling her as his last hope of reuniting with me. When she started her second semester of high school at her new Pittsburgh school, Jessa's guidance counselor arranged an introduction to a family counselor and potential friend. Christy turned out to be smart, motivated, pretty, and Heaven-sent. She immediately befriended Jessa. Jessa had zero interest in any Pittsburgh boy. She invited JB to the Snowball Dance, where the envious city boys mocked his mountain twang.

***

Wolf came to visit once three months after we moved, avowing his love and desire to change, clearly uneasy in the big city where he was sure I would soon be mugged. He was nervous outside of my rental home when riding in my car. He disdained the local accents, the higher prices, and the quicker pace of life. He was incredulous that I had left his mansion and his bed. I made it very clear to Wolf that I was not leaving my new home or my new job. My kids and I were settled into city life and loving it.

Liz, my dear friend from my first marriage, visited me more and was happier. She now lived in Wheeling, less than an hour away. We planned on celebrating my upcoming birthday by going to dinner downtown. Both of us were forty-one years old. She was still a stunning, petite beauty.

As a gift to myself, I scheduled a visit with Jill to get my light brown hair styled. After I told Jill of Wolf's recent visit, she asked, "So, are you, or are you not, divorcing this husband? This does not sound like the man for you. Just what are you looking for in a guy?"

"Let's see," I said, admiring my freshly coifed hair in her mirror. "At least six feet tall with good teeth. Don't care what he does, but he has to love his job."

I thought for a moment, then continued, "A Christian who lives his faith, with a dry sense of humor rather than goofy, and preferably a father, so he knows how to help me raise my kids."

Then, I said with conviction that I had placed my order.

Jill was quiet for ten seconds, a rarity, and then she announced, "There's this pilot, Ryan. He sings bass in a church choir. I will give him your number tonight and tell him to call you."

I waited. No call came. On the eve of my birthday, Liz called. She suddenly learned that she would have to work that night. Wow. All alone on my birthday. If only I had a date. Hmm.

The children were all spending the night with friends. I next remember the phone book in my hand. There were columns of numbers under "R. Davis." The project took me back to Warrington when I sat with Sharon; we had confidently gone down phone book columns and telemarketed our product with confidence. I had this down pat.

"Is your name Ryan? Are you a pilot? And is Jill your hairdresser?" I asked repeatedly.

Finally, I found an R. Davis who answered "yes" to all three questions. Jackpot!

"Well! I am the woman you are supposed to be calling!" I said in a measured cadence.

Brief, awkward conversation ensued—something about his schedule and his son visiting.

He was no Prince Charming on the phone. I didn't expect a call back. Afterward, I sat for a few more moments on my front porch, hearing the trolley pass through. I said out loud to only myself, "What a silly thing that was to do on my part!"

An unusual business trip followed the next weekend. It allowed Fern and Ford to accompany me. We stayed in the home of an actual heiress. Her father and brother were famous tycoons, yet she was one of my meagerly paid branch managers. She had married a paraplegic and devoted her life to helping the disabled. We were guests in her estate, where we discussed the needs of her region. Her home was filled with original art from the masters: O'Keefe, Renoir, Monet, Picasso, Van Gogh. These signatures from my art history class surrounded us. Fern, Ford, and I ate at her kitchen table, where she spoon-fed her husband. It wasn't her fortune I envied. She impressed upon us a living lesson on love.

There was much to tell Jessa when we returned. But before I could, she said, "Oh, Mom, that pilot called. His message is saved on the answering machine."

After pushing "Play," a sexy bass voice asked me to phone him back. I quickly did so.

After some initial pleasantries, I asked him, "Do you like being a pilot?"

"What other job pays you to talk to your friends and look out the window at clouds?" he replied. I could hear the smile in his voice, as he talked more about his professional life. It was clear to me that he really did love flying.

Okay, I thought, *this blind date is gonna happen.*

"Let's meet for coffee tomorrow," I told him. "Come to my office on Washington Road at three."

He was there on time, and he just made the cut at six feet. He had a masculine, Welsh look—a sort of Liam Neeson- or Richard Gere-type in my mind's movie. Oddly he wore his uniform pants and shoes with a golf shirt. He noticed my kids' photos on my desk and asked about their names. He looked slightly amused when I told him of my unusual choices.

"And *your* kids' names and ages?"

"Sarah and Adam are in their early twenties but Jacob just turned sixteen."

"What…Biblically traditional names," I said. "Mine have traditional middle names, so if they don't like their first names, they can be Marie, Peg, and Bob," I said as we left for coffee.

Minutes later, I told the barista, "The mocha mint latte with a crystallized candy stirrer."

Ryan pulled a can of plain iced tea, the kind that didn't even have lemon, from the cooler. We were *very* different.

For our second date, we went to a baseball game at Three Rivers Stadium. I wore red suede boots, new jeans, and a midriff top with my belly button making a special appearance. Having no interest in the game, I barraged him with questions. I needed to know if his mama was an alcoholic. That was where I had gone wrong in the past.

I opened with, "My parents are affectionate, always kissing and hugging. Was your mom a hugger?"

"She really wasn't. My parents aren't affectionate," he said.

This is sad, I thought. "Well, tell me what they *are* like."

The ball bounced back into his dugout.

"Very conservative. Their life is their work with the Gideons. You know, Bibles."

"Oh! Does that mean they are teetotalers?" I almost gushed with relief.

"Mom has never taken a drink in her life and Dad abstained after his Navy service years," Ryan said, with his eyes more on the game than on me. Was he nervous or afraid he'd miss a hit?

Bingo. Box checked. At least it seemed probable alcoholism would not rear its ugly head.

"I really prefer theater over sports," I said, trying not to sound too excited. "Did you know *Miss Saigon* is coming to town?"

"Well, if you don't piss me off, I might take you," he said, bouncing his knee rapidly.

He didn't seem to be joking, so I clammed up, thinking, *You just pissed* me *off, mister, enough to not date* you *again.*

"How long have you been divorced?" he asked, finally breaking the silence.

"Actually, tomorrow is my fourth anniversary. My divorce is final next week. Would you mind getting me a hot dog and some ice cream?" I asked.

He mercifully left me to absorb all that had happened.

"Is he your husband?" asked two men seated behind me.

"Oh, no. This is a first date," I answered, surprised.

"Ditch him! Meet us at Primanti Brothers after the game."

Though tempted, I declined.

Ryan returned with my dinner. The Pirates won in a record short game. No fireworks.

***

The next week, I flew to New England for a business retreat. Sharon and I had not seen each other since our high school reunion, four years ago. I arranged my work schedule carefully so that I had precious needed time to spend with my oldest friend.

"How did your date with the pilot go?" she asked.

"He was not my type. Too nervous. No more dates with him," I told her with certainty.

After I returned home, two important pieces of mail arrived: a signed divorce decree and a letter from Ryan thanking me for our ballpark date. I called Mom and read his letter to her.

Ryan had written, "Would you care to join me at the next game, this time with your children?"

"Give this guy another chance," my mother said. "Men don't write letters like that anymore."

On that date, he showed no signs of nerves. By chance, we ran into my old attorney, Ian, who later called me to discuss the date.

"I don't think he's the one for you," Ian said, dejectedly.

But Ryan became the strategic victor. At the game, he handed Fern and Ford a twenty each and told them to buy anything they wanted. Eyes wide, Fern tugged on my hand, whispering, "Mom, if this one asks you to marry him, say yes!" She was awed by his generosity.

"But I'm not in love with him, sweetheart," I whispered back.

She sighed sadly. "When will that happen, Mom?"

She wanted to know at that very moment. But it did happen, unexpectedly, in May on Ryan's forty-third birthday, four weeks after our first date.

"What's the most romantic restaurant in Pittsburgh?" I asked a new neighbor.

"That's an easy one to answer. The Hyeholde, out by the airport. But make reservations."

So, I made reservations and told Ryan that this dinner was my birthday gift to him. We sat at a private table in front of a huge window overlooking what looked like a lush fairy garden.

"Ryan, you have to make a toast," I said as my wine glass was raised on that special date.

"May all your shooting-star wishes come true," he said, smiling. "I'm honored to be with a woman such as you."

That night I fell in love with Captain Ryan.

CHAPTER TEN

Homerun Fireworks

Every week we went to another Pirates game. We invited Adam, Ryan's eldest son, to one. Father and son had reunited after months of not speaking after Adam traded college for a life of partying. Adam was a bit cocky, obviously amused over his dad's unexpected new girlfriend.

I still had not met Ryan's adopted daughter Sarah, who attended a religious affiliated college. I did meet Jacob, his younger son, a junior at a nearby high school. Jacob was interested in writing, theater, and playing the cello and had an effeminate nature. He definitely aligned himself with his mother. He was nothing like his navy-trained, conservative, masculine father. Ryan regretted raising his kids in the ultra-conservative church of his first wife, which he had since left. It turned them off to religion, he explained, with its narrowed focus of adopting the practices of the first century Christians, not to mention the certainty that only *their* church members were going to Heaven. Ryan now attended a Methodist church with an open mindset.

On that first meeting, Jacob casually asked me what I did for a living.

"Dance in bars," I shot back, straight-faced, while Ryan dropped to the floor in laughter.

The tension in this father-son relationship needed to be eased at any given opportunity.

***

About this time in Harrisburg, I attended a lunch with a famous author in the disability movement. The author listened as I told him of my diligence in supporting my regional managers and courting voting council members. His next cautionary words to me were prophetic. "The hardest part of your job will be dodging the bullets of your own troops. You have board members who are impossible to please. You are doing a standout job. Just keep it up," he cautioned.

It was common knowledge to all but me that one of my office managers was having an affair with my boss Ben. She had been threatened by my single status when I said casually to her, that "Ben is a big teddy bear." He *was* literally her teddy bear; thus, she had undue influence over my future. Soon after I made that comment, I found myself on an unofficial corrective action plan to be more "proactive" with no definition of what the term meant in relation to my job description. That experience did, however, teach me that office politics are dirty.

Proactively, after our first month of dating, Ryan said, "It is time to discuss the M word."

"Sure, I am all for monogamy," I coyly laughed. By now he was coming over daily.

"Not *that* M word. I am talking about marriage!" he said, as if I were completely clueless.

"My divorce was just finalized. I'm not getting married!" I was in total shock at this idea.

"If you do not marry me, I will stop seeing you," he said with an air of total confidence.

"You are tricking me into marriage!" I protested, then thought, *Should surrender come this easily?*

He had a stubborn, competitive nature. I had met my match. My fears of marrying a third time with six children and four aging parents between us were merited. Yet here was a man with loving eyes, a caring heart, worldly intelligence, and a deep Christian faith. This spiritual component was what had been missing in my previous marriages. I married first for physical attraction and second for blinding ambition. Before me was a tall, handsome, former aircraft carrier attack pilot with the goal of one day flying people across the Atlantic to European hubs.

But this man's biggest asset was the desire to hold my hand and pray with me—for our marriage, for our children, and for our world. He was shy and humble around people he didn't know. But he wanted more than anything to spend time talking to me every day that he wasn't flying. He talked of his travels to all seven continents and of his desire to take me and all of our children to see amazing places. Unlike my previous husbands, he knew what it was like to be an involved, divorced parent of three. His children were the same ages as my own when his ex-wife said to him, "While you were flying, we had a meeting and decided we want you to move out."

Ryan flew airplanes across the country while his ex raised the kids. They aligned themselves with their mom, when she simply fell out of love with dad. He stayed involved in their lives, despite her efforts to keep him from doing so. I hoped his kids would be happy for their dad, who was about to enter a marriage much healthier than the one they had seen him pushed from.

I could not turn down Ryan's proposal. I was in love with a role-model of trustworthiness and honesty, who would indeed take wonderful care of us and fly us off to magical places around the globe. I was in love with a faithful servant of God, who already prayed for four new souls he wanted to help protect.

And if you think my previous marriages happened quickly…. Ryan invited our children and me to yet another Pirates' game. We took the ferry across to Three Rivers Stadium on a perfect July fourth weekend.

At the end of the second inning, Ryan said, "Look at the Jumbotron!"

We all looked up at these huge streaming yellow letters:

LEIGH,
WILL YOU MARRY ME?
RYAN

The Pirates' parrot mascot appeared with roses and kissed me on camera. Ryan got down on one knee and….

"She said 'yes'!" he screamed to the cameraman. The crowd applauded around us. He placed a diamond and sapphire ring on my finger and his kiss rivaled the parrot's.

We signed a year lease on a stone house as we planned our wedding day, eighty-seven days from when we met. My favorite board member, an ordained minister, agreed to marry us. We met with him beforehand and visited a local church, yet the ceremony was in the backyard of our rental home on a corner lot in our town. There were twenty-five friends and relatives present. On our wedding day, I met my in-laws for the first time, who struck me as short, plain, quiet, and conservative. I'd already met Ryan's brother Jon and sister Audrey. Their mother, Ruth, asked them to prescreen me to see if Ryan had lost his mind. She knew he never made decisions on *anything* this fast.

Sarah, Ryan's daughter, made the road trip from Nashville where she attended college. She exposed her strained relationship with Ryan when she left our house in a tantrum after Ryan asked her to turn down a radio. Sarah had been adopted at age twelve. Ryan's ex felt a real loss at not having a daughter. Their solution for this was to go to an orphanage in Texas with their religious affiliation and bring into their home a girl born in the same year as their oldest son. Adam said it was as though their family was a perfect puzzle and suddenly a piece was being jammed between the cracks—a piece that did not at all fit in his mind. Sarah's birth family had placed four of their children up for adoption when their fifth child was born. Sarah's first adoptive father, a minister in Montana, had pushed the children's heads in the toilet when they misbehaved. When *the children* acted out following his abuse, he brought them back to Texas. Sarah was earning A's in school after all that had happened to her. She had real potential. Ryan promised Sarah that he would always be there for her, and he has been. That did not mean the adoption had been easy on the family. It began an eruption of rolling anger, raining down the lava of addictions and divorce.

At least my daughter Jessa was ecstatic over our upcoming wedding, but that was only because her boyfriend, JB, was her escort, visiting for her fifteenth birthday that same week. Liz was my maid of honor, and Ryan's only brother was our best man. Our children also stood with us for the short ceremony under young red oak trees, which provided much-needed shade in the summer heat. Adam was our only child not in attendance. He did not want to miss a Phish concert. His selfishness foreshadowed his cycles of addiction yet to come. He could not comprehend his dad finding happiness with a new wife, although his mother had found a new partner. Addiction often stunts emotional maturity.

By now, I'd had my fill of addiction with my exes. Ryan hadn't gotten the gene, but perhaps his children had. His ex-wife's brother battled alcoholism until his death, as did Ryan's maternal uncle. It was probable one of my own kids would get the dreaded gene. All I could do was pray that we'd get through whatever came our way, as a loving, married couple and family.

Following our wedding ceremony, we all went to an Italian restaurant chain for a casual reception. No big fuss. His parents refused to toast us, as it could *appear* they were drinking, despite the Pepsi poured into their glasses. This response to a wedding toast was a first for me.

Ryan should have told me earlier the pilot's motto, "Marry me and fly for free." That evening we sat in the first-class section of a late-night flight bound for Burlington, Vermont, with no time to change out of my wedding dress. We had a three-day honeymoon, staying first at a bed and breakfast and then at Shelburne Farms, a refurbished Vanderbilt estate in the countryside. We took an hour out of our honeymoon to hike Mt. Stowe with Sharon, my childhood friend who lives in the area. Sharon had never married and marveled that I had taken this chance so quickly. But she did not live with three impressionable children. Ryan vowed to be my husband and their father, for better or for worse, in sickness and in health. I hoped that this time, it really would be for as long as we both shall live.

I married a man, not solely for his good looks or ambition, but for his heart. This was my third time at bat. We would love each other with passion and loyalty in a strong, enduring marriage. And, he took me to the theater to see *Miss Saigon* after we returned. Apparently, I didn't piss him off too much.

CHAPTER ELEVEN
Ahead in the Count

After our honeymoon, I discovered painful uterine fibroid tumors were my new problem. My doctor said that exercise might help me get in better shape to combat this diagnosis, so Jessa and I joined a local karate school. Friends there told me it was not too late to tackle a black belt, which became my new long-term goal. This goal kept me occupied on weekends when Ryan usually flew airplanes.

"My job is stressing me out," I said to him one day after he came back home. "It really helps to kick butt in karate class, but it seems like I'm always tired. With this job there are two buckets and the bucket of brown is outweighing the bucket of green."

"Listen, I enjoy my job, even when the flight attendants are mean and the hotel is crappy," he replied, wrapping his long, comforting arms around me and gazing into my eyes. "If your job is stressful, get out. Don't you realize you never have to worry about money again?"

"As a matter of fact, those are the sexiest words ever said to me. Could I offer my resignation?"

"I want only your happiness. It's time for you to get back into theater and art and music and do what you love doing," he said. "This is a no-brainer!"

Ridding myself of work stress, my full-time job titles became "pilot's wife" and "mom." We prioritized traveling together as a family, and we soon visited Sarah in Nashville, Jacob in Fort Myers, and the San Diego Zoo with Adam and my kids. Yet the challenges of blending two diverse families awaited us.

His parents' conservative lifestyle was my first surprise. When we visited them down south, we were treated to lunch at a barbecue restaurant. An aromatic basket of hushpuppies graced our table. These corn-flavored doughnut holes were never offered in northern restaurants. I raised one to my watering mouth.

"We have not blessed the hushpuppies!" my mother-in-law blurted out, eyes wide at me.

What would have happened if we hadn't? I thought.

Ryan had briefed me about them. Every childhood family vacation had centered around Gideon conventions. Democrats like me were seen as unsaved, and pro-choicers like me were surely damned to eternal hellfire.

While visiting, we took the short drive to Duke University, Ryan's alma mater. We snuck into Cameron Indoor Stadium, all alone in there, as spotlights shone on hallowed jerseys. Ryan was so ecstatic that he teared up. He was fanatical about Duke basketball. I had never been exposed to March Madness and honestly thought it was a musical about some mythical Mad March Hatter whom Alice had met in Wonderland. Ryan schooled me in Duke topics, like the arch rival Tarheels, choosing the correct darker blue hue, and which North Carolina conservative commentator dubbed rival town Chapel Hill "a fenced-in zoo."

Another obstacle was factoring in the parenting preferences of Ryan's ex. Ryan had been financially cheated by his ex, though he paid her exorbitantly when she chose to leave him. She was moving south with her wealthy husband and wanted Jacob to live with us. She expected Ryan to pay out-of-district fees for Jacob to remain in his current public school, yet she wouldn't pay *us* any support. So Jacob finished high school living with his mom in Florida after living with us for one summer.

In contrast to me telling my children to find a summer job at sixteen to learn the value of money, she said, "Jacob is not to work, as his cello is too important. His fingers need protecting."

Jessa landed a job at an ice cream parlor in a nearby mall. Fern worked there, too. Jacob followed the rules in our home, though, and got his first job stacking grocery shelves.

Still, Jacob seldom communicated his plans and broke the house rules by staying out late with our cars, knowing his dad wouldn't confront him. Ryan shared with me that as a preschooler, Jacob showed signs of identifying as a girl, preferring dolls and dresses. He was evaluated by Johns Hopkins Center for Sexual Orientation. They said he was destined to grow up to be an "effeminate homosexual." His ex's reaction was to pray and Ryan coached him in T-ball. Due to his sensitive nature, Jacob's parents never came down hard on him...about anything.

Then Adam asked Ryan for help to buy a used car. Ryan decided to take the money earmarked for his college and "sell" him our van. Adam had been through drug rehab twice by now, yet just after he got the van, his mother told us he was drinking heavily again. Ryan simply would not ask his sons confronting questions, and I could only lose by overstepping boundaries.

My own girls could not be more different from each other. Jessa was the overachieving honors student, bossy to a fault, who was All-American beautiful. Fern was the sweet, sensitive child, my affectionate, cute, silly girl. Kids teased her because of her large jaw. Never mind her skin, teeth, eyes, and hair were enviably lovely. She looked to me like a young Hillary Swank.

My social butterfly, Ford, loved sports and "only Italian girls." He could sell air with his charm. Ryan, however, did not emotionally connect to Ford. Ryan's own father had not connected to him growing up either. Ryan's relationships with his own sons were lacking, as nothing pushed his buttons worse than boys not toeing a straight line, just as he had done as the church-going boy scout and diligent student on a Navy ROTC scholarship.

In an effort to better blend our family of three boys and three girls, we rented a North Carolina beach house and invited our friends and our children's friends. Fern's best friend who joined us was Alice. She told us her dad was a pilot with the airline where Ryan worked. We soon realized that her mother had divorced her father, when he decided to become a woman. Our minds were opened to this family who needed compassion over the strain this change produced.

After a year of renting a home with antiquated plumbing and wiring, we were ready to buy our first home. Our bedroom had been an attic loft with no air conditioning, no door, and a cramped shower. We searched for a corner lot within walking distance of the high school. We bought a clinker brick cape cod, shaded by large trees and edged by stacked rock walls. We hoped to live there for decades with stellar schools, kind neighbors, and well-behaved kids.

Fern made another friend besides Alice. Days after her thirteenth birthday, Fern, who was trying to fit in, got caught shoplifting with this new friend at Sears. That incident caused our first worries about Fern's poor judgment, which we thought was due in part to her poor self-esteem.

A counselor told us once that part of the definition of addiction is separation. I could feel Fern separating herself from her family, but so subtly. After all, part of teen angst is separating from parents and gravitating toward peers. But, her self-image was not healthy.

Fern's orthodontist suggested we investigate jaw surgery. Her speech, bite, and identity were affected by her growing jaw, he explained. She inherited this trait from her father, whose jaw matched his large frame, and was more pleasing in a male's facial structure.

At sixteen, Jessa was finally warming up to the idea of having a Pittsburgh boyfriend. Football star Matt fell hard for her through their junior and senior years. He took her to every dance. He and Jessa's now best friend, Christy, persuaded her to audition for the marching band Rockettes dance team. Jessa made the team and a year later asked me, knowing the competition, "Do you think I should try for Rockette captain?"

"Jessa, you have always been a leader. You always get what you go after. Go for it."

Soon after giving this advice, I was sewing gold sequins on her dance captain's gloves.

***

Airlines operate every day of the year and, as usual, Ryan worked over Thanksgiving of 1998. I went with Sharon to my twenty-fifth high school reunion while my parents stayed with the kids. Age had been kind to my oldest friend. She was still single, still beautiful, with an enviable figure. She had persevered through much college debt to get her graduate degree and her counselor's license. She had recently opened her own business as a psychotherapist. It felt like old times to go to her childhood home and visit with her family. She had driven south from her home in Vermont and was able to be my chauffeur to the reunion. This time the reunion was held in a posh restaurant ball room with a live band.

Now divorced, my ex-beau Bobby took little time to ask me to dance. Curiosity got the best of me and we headed to the dance floor.

"You are even more beautiful than before. Please accept my apology for being such a jerk. Does your husband know how lucky he is?" my formerly shy boyfriend said, adding, "I cannot stop looking at you."

"The luck is mine, Bobby," I told him as we danced. "You can look all you want. You just can't touch these days."

CHAPTER TWELVE
Seventh Inning Stretch

Never was I happier than with my third choice of husbands. After my return, we learned my sister-in-law Audrey was going to marry *her* new beau, Tom. We both liked him enormously. The wedding would take place near where my first husband lived. I called to offer Jon visitation with his children, as a random act of kindness. An answering machine took my offer.

His wife called me back. "Jon chooses not to see them, as he feels too ashamed," she said.

After that phone call, I sat in a room by myself in quiet contemplation. Ryan was so very different from my previous husbands. Above all, he took a vested interest in raising our six children, imparting Christian values and ethics. We had discussions with the kids about handling money, sex, religion, and politics—all topics that can split relationships apart. We agreed on most of these values and ethics. Whenever a crisis arose, he was the cooler head, calming me and prioritizing with me, much as though he were in a cockpit managing an abnormal situation. He had one hard and fast rule, though: the children would be confirmed in our faith and attend Sunday church. We hoped that if we could impart a strong set of morals on the basis of faith, wiser decisions would follow.

But then we found that first pack of "cancer sticks" in Jacob's room, a room he shared with Ford. We confronted him and he countered with, "Mom's known of my smoking for the past four years!"

Well, if Mama condones it….

"Our mom provides cigarettes for her sons and smokes with them," Sarah then told us.

I called their mother, who was a dental hygienist, incredulous that she would advocate smoking for her teenage sons. Ryan listened, as he put off talking to his ex-wife at all costs.

"I only smoke one a week. I am not addicted," she told me, from within her smoky cloud of denial.

We told Jacob to quit, hoping to avoid his college allowance being wasted on cigarettes. Jacob often brought his best friend, Cory, to our home. Jessa loved this, as he was movie-star handsome, tall, blond, and suave. Then Ryan's ex phoned us with this prophetic warning: "Jacob must stop seeing Cory. He's a bad influence, smoking and selling pot. I called his mom to tell her he keeps a scale under his bed for his sales purposes, and she refused to look!"

My prayer was that we would never be ostrich parents like Cory's mom, with our heads buried in the sand.

***

Knowing it was time to start preparing Jacob and Jessa for college, we visited many colleges. Jacob chose a city university and was awarded a scholarship. Jessa chose an out-of-state university where she was awarded a scholarship. They were flying out of the nest to see the world! The family dynamic was shifting with Fern and Ford at home, now in their own rooms.

At the close of Jessa's junior year, she was still dating football star Matt, but she told me, "There's this guy in my homeroom named Jack, a football player, a big guy with these beautiful light blue eyes. And he stares at me. He's really shy and sweet, and I kind of like him. And his mom tells him every morning, 'Do something kind for someone today,' and he really tries to."

The next time her old friend Tanya visited from West Virginia, Jessa announced, "We want to go to the Southside on the trolley."

"No," I replied. "That's a much rougher neighborhood than where we live."

"Mom, Jack and his friends will be our bodyguards. They are all big football linemen."

At what is known as the "T station," I met my future son-in-law for the first time.

"Don't you leave their side, Jack," I said. He was shy and clearly love-stricken.

"Yes ma'am. My pleasure. Thank you. I promise you I will not take my eyes off her."

And he did not. Having had many dating relationships since going to my prom with Bobby, I couldn't imagine Jessa marrying one of her two high school beaus. My wish for her was that she'd make a better choice than I had, not rushing into a marriage destined for failure. Thankfully, a long courtship ensued. Sadly, she had seen too many tears of mine shed over her biological father and Wolf.

My children were finally seeing a healthy model of marriage. Ryan and I celebrated our second anniversary on the sixty-second floor of the US Steel Building. As soon as Ryan surprised me with a liquid silver necklace, fireworks exploded below us, as if on cue. The next day he took me on an overnight visit to New Orleans. Ryan's first officer and a flight attendant went to dinner with us on Bourbon Street. This female pilot would die years later in a single-vehicle accident. Our friends think Ryan is at greater risk flying a plane than they are going to work.

"Be afraid of accidents in cars, not planes," Ryan tells me. And accident statistics back him up.

***

The anniversary to be celebrated in grand style was my parents' fiftieth. We treated them and their three grandchildren to a vacation in Germany. We stayed at the Chiemsee Armed Forces Recreation Center, originally built by Hitler. Then we visited the eerily haunting Dachau concentration camp. We saw opulent castles, the elegant gardens of Salzburg, and ended with a stay in Oberammergau, famed for its *Passion Play* and nestled in the snow-covered Alps.

We rode the tram up the Zugspitze, the highest mountain in Germany, where Fern got a nosebleed from the altitude after we threw snowballs. We visited with Mom's German cousin, Martin, and his wife, whom I had last seen during my semester abroad. It was not easy keeping family members ages twelve through seventy-four happy, but we wanted my parents to enjoy a dream family vacation in their ancestral country, while celebrating a milestone. We succeeded.

***

In the first years of our marriage, our biggest argument was over my desire to get a dog. What a stark contrast from the volatile arguments over drugs and alcohol in my first marriages! Finally, Ryan gave me the go-ahead to look for a German shepherd, as one of his childhood friends had one, and he was envious at the time. In the fall of 1999, this local ad found me: "German shepherd one-year old male, all shots, AKC extremely gentle, kennel, 100 dollars."

We drove to a nearby town to bring home Rex, our loving guard dog for the next decade. As intelligent as he was, he was emotionally damaged from suffering abuse in his first home.

We were ever vigilant with our guard dog when strangers entered the front door, especially men.

***

Jack was trying harder and harder to woo Jessa away from Matt. Jack was awarded a full football scholarship to Vanderbilt University. He convinced Jessa we should visit the school with him and his mom. While the campus was lovely, the price tag was triple what we had budgeted. We told Jessa to apply anyway in case she wanted to transfer there after her freshman year.

Jessa dated both Jack and Matt that year. It was only natural to invite both to her graduation dinner at our home. Matt was relieved when Vanderbilt wait-listed her application, though Jack was more upset than Jessa. Jack played in the state East-West game coached by Mike Pettine, my old history teacher. What a small world! Before he left for summer football at Vanderbilt, Jack gave Jessa a dozen red roses and shed tears when they said their goodbyes. A month later I drove Jessa to college to room with Tanya, the same childhood friend who Wolf disliked for no reason, on a rainy, weepy day. Tanya was relieved to meet Jessa's new stepdad, Wolf now a distant memory.

But Wolf had been thinking of me. He had my old friend Maggie mail his letter to me, as he did not know my address. That was my first contact with him since our divorce four years before. Just opening the letter made me nervous. It was comprised of this one scrawled sentence:

"Accept the enclosed check in lieu of the property settlement, as time is money."

He followed-up with a phone call offering me double, asking if I knew the time value of money. I knew the value of hiring an attorney who got us what had been promised, minus his fee. Wolf bad-mouthed me throughout his small town, once telling outlandish lies to Tanya, who he drunkenly approached at a bar. Thank God, he was no longer a part of our lives.

***

Though Fern had not made the band flag team the year before, she persisted, tried again, and earned a spot on the flag team with Alice. At sixteen, she was starting to date. When the orthodontist removed her braces, we found an experienced oral surgeon to perform a jaw-bone reduction. The surgery would be complex and painful, but Fern was raring to go with hopes of softening her appearance and improving her self-esteem.

***

If marriage is a pot of soup, it seemed we were stirring a lot into it...or ladling out the bitter herbs. Kids going off to college meant more expenses. Upcoming surgery meant preparing for a homebound tutor. Hiring an attorney to deal with an ex was complicated. So when we traveled, it was like turning off the burner, putting a lid on it, and leaving the flavors to blend.

Our next getaway alone was a snorkeling adventure in Grand Cayman. We went on a charter boat to frolic with sting rays, a moray eel, and a five-foot shark. The boat broke down, much to my delight, and gave us extra time to play mermaid and merman in crystal aqua water.

We visited the town of Hell, where fragrant white jasmine vines covered lawns. We peeked in at Bill Gate's estate at the remote end of the isle. Getaways like this reinvigorated our marriage. We took advantage of the ability to fly at no cost to remote islands. This is what made our marriage unique. These mini-vacations did not cure our marital ills, but they bound us tighter.

After visiting Grand Cayman, Ryan was the best man in his brother's wedding and toasted the new couple with these words in front of every member of his large assembled family: "My wish for you is to be as happy as my wife and I!"

And then he kissed me. I melted, euphoric in our closeness.

CHAPTER THIRTEEN

Check the Runner

On Ryan's birthday, I surprised him with the gift of Will's sculpture of me called *The Dreamer*. It was sculpted at the height of our affair and was now reproduced and sold on his website and in catalogues. Will charged me a third of the catalog fee and included this message inside the carefully packed crate: "Happy Birthday Ryan. Your wife stole this from me. Enjoy!"

At the age of fifty, Will found himself joyfully marrying another artist half his age. He had, like me, finally found a life-mate who made him whole. Looking back, I realized that Will and I were too similar, two creative, passionate souls with birthdays less than a week apart. Our zodiac animal is the ram and our element is fire. Horns would have locked, our fire flaming out under the marital pressures of a blended family. But Ryan was my opposite, a Gemini. His element is air, and it is there where he is most comfortable, flying me high literally and figuratively, a calming influence.

Ryan realized his dream of flying passengers across the Atlantic to London, Paris, Frankfurt, and Rome. Since he'd come to know London well, Jessa and I went along on two of his back-to-back trips. We stayed over while he flew to Pittsburgh and then returned to pick us up. While waiting for his return, we visited with my cousin Jean and her mother, Peggy. This would be the last time to see Peggy, age eighty-five, before her death. She lived in what once was a mint to a castle lord in medieval times. She treated us to formal tea in Stratford's Old George Hotel.

Following this trip, we had a unique Thanksgiving holiday with Fern and Ford in Germany. Both were taking German in school and lovingly remembered their nana Marie, so they enjoyed the cultural experience. The hotel was in a seventeenth-century fort on the Rhine River, where the staff generously cooked up the American traditional turkey feast for the airline crews. Not too many children can say their father took them to a Thanksgiving celebration in Mainz, Germany, over their long weekend break.

***

I visited Sharon, and we celebrated forty years of friendship. She was searching for financial gain, her soul mate, and self-actualization via an Indian guru. Talking about faith in Jesus was not "progressive." Was I regressive, I wondered, or were we worlds apart? She had returned from working in an ashram in India. While there she told of being on a bus that stopped for a bathroom break by a field of mangos. And there, by the side of a road, she said she felt a presence of divine inspiration and love surrounding her. Despite our vast theological differences, my prayers continue for my childhood friend to find the prince and the peace she truly believed awaited her.

My old friend Liz, who first met me over her husband's fraudulent insurance claim, was the heir of her childless aunt. Liz was shocked when the aunt's neighbor called to say that not only had the aunt died, but she was quickly buried just after making the neighbor sole heir in an altered sizeable will. Liz hired an attorney, and Ryan and I attended the trial in rural Ohio. The county prosecutor felt it was likely the aunt had been poisoned, though it was never proven, yet justice prevailed in finding the new will to be a forgery. Liz collected her inheritance minus the hefty lawyers' fees. She moved into her aunt's modest home on a rural Ohio road, yards away from the suspected murderess. She purchased new cars for herself and her children and created a cozy new home for herself with lavish gardens.

Not only was Ryan supportive of me in stressful times, but he was also empathic to my old friend, praying for her and providing her with a loan to cover her trial attorney retainer. He knew that if Liz lost her case, the debt may not have been paid. She had stood with us at our wedding. Now, she needed help. He cared. This act of kindness on his part solidified my marriage.

***

It was easier to guide our friends through stressful times than to deal with our own. Adam's mother visited him in his Pittsburgh apartment and found him nearly dead on the floor from combining cocaine with vodka. I realized that Ryan had become the ostrich parent I had feared. He refused to confront his sons when they had obvious life-threatening problems. Adam was accepted into an inpatient rehab that cost thousands. His mother split the bill with us.

Jacob lost his scholarship due to his poor grades. Ryan did not ask questions. Jacob's handsome friend, Cory, whose mother had ignored the scale found under his bed, was found dead from an overdose following rehab. In reaction to this tragedy, Jacob's drug use increased.

Discussions arose with my own three over the real possibility of one of them facing addiction someday. They saw my open fear of this future, versus how Ryan hid his fears from all of us. Ryan was strong in many ways, but he was afraid to face the addictions and corresponding manipulations of his own sons. He was fallible after all. At least he confessed his failures to God.

***

Ryan told our new minister of my theater degree and experience. Our minister's wife headed up the drama troupe. I spent many Sunday nights acting in or directing liturgical dramas before the sermons. Ryan and I had joined a large church. There, within this small drama team, I met my best Pittsburgh friend, Earla, who was about to divorce a troubled man with whom she had two great kids. A Marcia Clark look-alike, she was a gifted actress and remains a close friend. She later remarried a man who brought her long-deserved joy. We have that blessing in common.

Early in 2001, Fern had her long-anticipated surgery, which lasted more than four hours. Her upper and lower jaws were sawed clean through, readjusted, and wired shut. I slept in her hospital room, amazed at her bravery and strength through such trauma. Our young minister, Eric, said a healing prayer at her side, and it was answered. Within six weeks, she went to her first dance on a date. Soon after, she acted in school plays, went from the flag team to the Rockette dance team, attended Young Life Camp with the church choir, and toured colleges with the plan of becoming an elementary school teacher. We acted together in a church dinner theater benefit playing mother and daughter. As she grew in beauty and confidence, it seemed we were growing closer. I treasure my memories of this time. It was as if I were admiring the peaceful beauty of a mountaintop lake...just before the dam breaks. History tells us this actual tragic event happened long ago in the city of Johnstown, Pennsylvania, a short drive away from where we lived.

Pastor Eric confirmed and mentored Ford at age fourteen. My parents attended this time, to see the minister lay hands on my sweet son, blessing him. He began to apply himself academically, earning a place among the honor roll. His activities centered around playing on the lacrosse team. We treated him to an enrollment at Duke University lacrosse camp as a reward.

We also visited Duke for Ryan's twenty-fifth reunion. Following a classy banquet, the Drifters played by the dance floor, and then we were treated to lavish fireworks. Ryan ran into a man he didn't recognize.

"Ryan, don't tell me you don't remember who you shared a bed with in Perth!" He was an old Navy pal who had married a Duke alumna.

They had indeed shared a bed when a group of young naval officers had one week's leave from the *USS America* in 1981. They sprang for the royal suite of the Hilton. Catching up with a sea service buddy was an unexpected treat.

This experience contrasted heavily with the filthy campus lodgings and chicken dinner at my college reunion. The unexpected plus there was visiting with my friend, Gary, the vessel commander of the New Jersey State Police Newark Port Station. President Bush honored my college friend for his bravery on 9/11 with a citation. Gary led his troopers to work with him for two days, shuttling victims across the Hudson River to safety. Gary surprised his old college girlfriend Joy and me with private access to Lady Liberty, which was then closed to the public. He took us by boat to a guard who welcomed us to the statue's entrance. At the top of Lady Liberty's crown, Joy and I giggled as we kissed our hero from each side. Through all this excitement, Ryan stayed behind at the port state police station in Gary's padded office chair, due to a pulled back muscle.

***

At age nineteen, Jessa received her official acceptance into Vanderbilt University. Jack told us, "I prayed like I never prayed before." Her heart now belonged to him. He gave her a diamond-and-gold heart necklace, and then he told Ford privately, "I *will* marry your sister."

***

I made a chilling discovery while Ryan was flying. Jacob left a box of books by our computer. The top book was his journal. I could not resist opening it. It told of his frequenting gay bars as his feminine persona, as well as detailing his addiction to Ecstasy and Oxycodone, two often-fatal drugs. But the worst part was that the pages were full of pure venom toward us: "She's my nemesis, the step monster," and "I'll never become the monster that is my dad."

Ryan's response to this discovery was to join Jacob on a walking trail to tell him, "I know of your homosexual orientation. I still love you. And now we need to discuss your drug use." Jacob downplayed the answer on that topic. It seemed both father and son avoided confrontation.

Ford told me when Jacob lived with us the previous summer, he had taken a bong from their shared room onto a plane to Florida. Ford was afraid to tell Ryan, fearing he would "shoot the messenger," a recurring pattern in step-parenting.

After the walk Ryan and Jacob had, Ryan's ex called to say that Adam had again relapsed with a drinking and driving incident. And, she added, concerning her younger son, "Jacob needs rehab because problems do not go away due to frank talks on trails."

Adam soon took us away from worries over Jacob, who at least was returning to college. When we were visiting Vanderbilt for a home football game, Sarah called late into the night.

"Adam attempted suicide at mom's home and there was blood everywhere from where he cut his wrists," she cried into the phone. "He was so high and belligerent when police came, he had to be put into a straightjacket!"

I discovered that Ryan had written Adam a large check, despite my protesting Ryan enabling his son. Ryan was now shooting me, the messenger, at my suggestion that his overly generous check had led to this terrible moment.

***

We made two decisions that helped solidify our marriage. One, I began to earn my own wages again, this time as a substitute teacher for Pittsburgh schools. I became a sought-after sub for my favorite elementary school. I landed full-time gigs, working when I wished with kids who were familiar with me. Two, we entered into marriage counseling. Perhaps my recent earning of a black belt in Tai Kwan Do strengthened my character. I broke my boards with a jumping 360-degree back kick. Karate became my channel for the frustration I felt watching Ryan being manipulated toward such hurtful outcomes. With both of his sons using dangerous, illegal drugs, we needed to bounce our marital differences by a professional.

At our first marriage counseling session, our therapist asked Ryan what had attracted him to me, besides anything physical. He did not hesitate to answer, "She was honest and open from the start, with no hidden agendas."

He continued, smiling at me, "She was so comfortably confident that she sang love songs aloud to me in my car when we first met. We had the same outlook on life. We made faith and family our priorities, rather than materialism."

The counselor applauded our romantic time away together to work on undoing our strains. We could not fix our children, but we could fix how we dealt with them by forming a united front—and having lots of great sex.

***

We took full advantage of our airline travel benefits over the next six months. We visited Wiesbaden, Germany, to see Roman baths and the Frauenstein castle built in 1180. We cruised the Rhine to the town of Koblenz. We relaxed *au naturel* at the hotel spa. We visited cousin Jean again, as we enjoyed a walking tour of London's Heaths. We rented another beach house with our kids and our dog, Rex. We visited Ocean City, Maryland, to see the wild ponies at Assateague Island National Seashore. We saw my college pal Joy when we took in a Duke basketball game at the Meadowlands. We drove to West Virginia to see my friend Maggie marry a fellow professor and to visit with old friends. This travel was a huge ingredient of our marriage therapy.

Were it not for the counseling sessions, our travels, and our constant prayers, our marriage would have ended. Stepparenting always brings tension to a marriage, as it pulls on the loyalty strings of the heart. Ryan's *modus operandi* was to shut down emotionally, while I needed to talk things through. Our marriage counselor was struck by our opposite coping skills. She applauded our efforts at mini-vacations and said she often recommended couples take in regular Saturday-night dates or weekend sojourns. In our unique relationship, Ryan worked on weekends, when he flew routes that changed every month. I became a sort of hitchhiker in the sky on his longer work trips. It was no trouble at all to fly for free, most of the time. But very soon, an event would change airline travel forever, for everyone.

CHAPTER FOURTEEN
Rain Delay

Ryan flew south to support Adam who had just been discharged from rehab. Ryan returned home exhausted on a late-night flight. The next morning, he deeply needed to sleep in.

"Ryan, are you still asleep? Your mom is on the phone. She says there's a plane crash all over the news. She has a lot of questions that I cannot answer."

"I am so tired. Turn on the television. Tell me all about it when I wake up," he mumbled.

"Ryan, this plane crashed into the World Trade Center tower," I said more insistently, interrupted his sleep again.

Up in an instant, he later journaled, "9-11: The day the world changed. Numb, stunned, tears, sobbing grief. Phone calls all day. Disbelief. All flights to anywhere cancelled or diverted."

"My gut tells me I will know a pilot who died today," he said, staring at the TV screen.

His intuition was correct. His naval reserve commanding officer was non-revenue flying that day, which means that he was utilizing free flying privileges as an airline employee. A recently retired airline captain, Wilson "Bud" Flagg and his wife were two of the passengers flown into the Pentagon on 9/11. Ryan resolved to become a Federal Flight Deck Officer in memory of Rear Admiral Flagg. These pilots are trained on their own dime and time to ensure safe flight decks. Ryan provided this thankless, uncompensated service for the next ten years.

The economic losses to his employer were the worst in the airline industry. Their Washington, D.C. hub was closed for twenty-three days before gradually reopening. This eventually resulted in bankruptcy, a 40-percent loss in pilot salaries, the government buying out pensions, and the lowest commercial pilot salaries nationwide. We saw the effects of 9/11 on Vegas two months later when we stayed there at a deeply discounted rate. We never stood in lines or pushed through the usual crowds. Sin City was a ghost town, as folks were afraid to fly.

***

After a depressing eight months for Ryan, the airline industry, and the nation, I decided to surprise Ryan with a birthday dinner at the same restaurant where he had proposed five years earlier. We sat at the same table. I wore the same red dress. Marriage counseling was working.

Days before, I received a surprise check in the mail for my child support in arrears. After learning of my first mother-in-law's death, I was smart enough to research putting a lien on the estate through my child support representative. A state-appointed attorney kept tabs on my first husband's inheritance. The lawyer recommended we attend the family court hearing, especially after we told him about our free flying benefit.

"Where in the world is your office from the Charlotte airport?" I asked the attorney.

"Head south on the interstate for a half hour and take Cherry Road exit south," he directed me.

When Ryan and I arrived at family court in the deep south, there Jon sat in the waiting room. He was missing his front teeth, balding, and hunched over with many weathered wrinkles. After we greeted him, he looked directly up into my face, confused, and said, "Ahm sorry, Ah don't know you ma'am."

Was this the result of his brain on drugs?

"Well, that's interesting, since we have three kids together." *I* hadn't changed *that* much!

"Ah nevah expected to see you heah," he stammered in his feigned southern accent.

"I am sure you did not. Here are some pictures of the kids."

I left current photos of his children with him out of pure pity. Their preferred father—our protector and provider—sat by me quietly, looking years younger than Jon. In fact, Ryan was two months older. I had not chosen well the first time, but finally did so on the third try. The result of this hearing was the check I received in the mail—Jon's entire inheritance yet thousands less than he owed me for child support. The judge closed the case. We never thought we would return to that sleepy little college town in South Carolina again. How wrong we were.

When we were married almost six years, we flew south again to celebrate my in-laws' fiftieth anniversary with a banquet reception. We attended their country church the next morning with the entire family. Ryan stressed how vital it was for all of their grandchildren to attend, yet Jacob failed to catch the trolley from his dorm downtown in time for his ride to the airport.

Fern and Ford joined us on a Windjammer cruise out of St. Maarten. Ford and Ryan crewed the *Stars and Stripes* yacht, winning a race. It was wonderful to see them bonding through this memorable activity. We stopped at Montserrat to see its active volcano spewing ash into the air. Quite by coincidence, we had a private tour of the island from the minister of tourism. While we swam, our snorkeling guide took a baby octopus out of its lair as it spurted an inky cloud around us. It clung to my arm as we snorkeled off of St. Kitts. We saw the Southern Cross constellation "for the first time," as the song goes. I caught two baby sharks off the stern. The stirring tradition of this tall wooden sailing ship was to raise its sails while the crew played "Amazing Grace" through loudspeakers across the deck. Listening to this sacred hymn, written in 1772 by a newly converted sailor who came to see slavery as despicable, brought tears to the eyes of everyone on board.

Jessa accompanied us on a working trip to Paris in 2004. We three climbed the Eiffel Tower and took an open-air bus tour amidst the blooms of April. Ryan knew the perfect bistro with the smoothest Beaujolais wine. We marveled at the architecture, the kissing couples everywhere, and artists painting their canvases on sidewalks along ornate bridges.

These were precious travels with the children before they grew into busy adults with their own families and schedules.

***

Ford's high school sweetheart was Penny. She looked like a teenaged Jennifer Aniston. She was a star volleyball player, petite, blonde, and sassy. She was a foot shorter than Ford, as he had shot up to nearly six foot in height. We all adored her until the relationship ran its course. Ford and Penny experienced young love together, and all my Penny memories are good ones…even when they admitted to me that they were having sex. Penny told me, though, that if I told her mom, she'd be killed, and Ford assured me they were using birth control. It opened the door for an honest relationship with my only son. This girlfriend was a much-needed younger sister to Fern. They bonded immediately and enjoyed being together.

Yet, Fern was beginning to show serious signs of defiance. When she took our cars out much later than her curfew, we attributed this to what we deemed a pattern of bad decisions: cigarettes, marijuana, drinking, and we suspected, casual sex. We tried to show our love for her by giving her a combination of a pre-prom party at home, a graduation dinner party, and an eighteenth birthday joint celebration with Penny at a favorite restaurant. Because these gestures were ineffective, we found a counselor over the summer who was a mere short-term fix. When Fern came home sulking, I wanted to hide, not seeing a positive outcome and totally at a loss as to what to do. Fern's new summer job at the country club where her sister worked had her tagging along with a new friend named Brittany, though we did not meet her that first summer.

Because Fern and Ford were so close in age, we took them both to visit prospective colleges for Fern. Ryan had been bringing me home bath bombs from a posh shop in London. On a lark, we rented hotel rooms in the vicinity of the colleges we would tour the next day and we took along one of these bombs in our luggage. What we didn't realize is that when we emerged from the tub the night before, there were tiny bright specks of gold glitter all over us. Oddly enough, this gold dust only appeared when the sun was shining brightly on Ryan's face, such as when we met with the dean of the college that following beautiful, sunlit morning. My very masculine former Navy attack pilot had a good laugh explaining his sparkling skin to the curious dean.

In fact, Fern chose that college. She chose it for its reputable teacher education program. We were glad that Fern joined the college band as a flag girl. We were grateful for her roommate, Mel, who became a valuable friend. We were pleased that Fern pledged a sorority. Soon, she was thriving in her small-town college life.

Jessa finished her undergraduate requirements a semester early, just as I had years ago. She applied to nursing school with the goal of becoming a pediatric nurse practitioner. She planned to begin in the fall on her own dime. Until then, she worked as a substitute teacher, living at home.

Meanwhile, Jack stayed busy playing football at Vanderbilt University. He was chosen to be the first junior ever elected as team captain, retaining the leadership position as a senior.

***

I joined a book club of Carnegie librarians with my friend Earla from the drama team at church. We took turns researching books. My first assigned book told of the Johnstown, Pennsylvania floods. Ryan and I decided a day trip there would add depth to my research. We spent hours on the road touring the town, museum, and dams and visiting the minister who married us. We never thought we would ever visit that infamous town again. Oh, if only *that* were true! Three short years from now, Fern would get stuck in this infamous dammed and damned city in the biggest rut of her life.

We were surprised to get a call from Jacob asking for help to move out of his dorm permanently and into his mother's home. He was attending outpatient drug rehab, and we were to ship him his belongings. He had not shown up for exams nor handed in assignments for courses, so he failed. In effect, we had wasted thousands on college tuition. For once, Ryan saw to it that consequences followed and gave Jacob the remaining payment coupons on his college loan. Ryan informed him that he would be responsible for the remaining debt. Fortunately, Jacob realized the importance of education and completed college later by paying for it himself. He had an epiphany about the importance of finishing his degree whereas sadly two of our children would not…and they went on to reap the consequences.

***

At the year's end, we created a Christmas card list. It was time to reconnect with Dr. Paul and send him a photo of my children, all of whom he delivered. I phoned his office.

"I want to send a card to Dr. Paul and his family. Do I still have his correct address?"

"Oh," the receptionist replied, falling silent for a moment. "The doctor passed away suddenly from a heart attack in August. I am so sorry."

A memory came to mind of him once telling me this was exactly how his father had died. I sent a card to his wife with a favorite photo of him after Ford's birth. One of my heroes was dead in midlife, and it shocked me to my core. Dr. Paul was one of the kindest, most intelligent men I had ever known. He lived right, doing everything he was supposed to do, but he possessed a bad role of the gene dice and could not escape a short life on this earth. I thought of my first husband, whose own father had literally dropped dead of a heart attack in his front yard at the age of fifty-two. I pray that my son does not inherit that set of genes through his biological father.

CHAPTER FIFTEEN
Time Out

It was Ryan's health that became an issue in 2004, when a rare condition developed. We planned to rendezvous at the Charlotte airport, and then go to dinner with his sister, Audrey, and her husband, Tom. Ryan greeted me looking confused and ashen.

"Something's wrong. I feel dizzy. I'm having balance difficulties," he said, and I saw him sway slightly on his legs. "Maybe I ate something bad because I may vomit. You go out with Audrey and Tom, but I'm going to bed at the hotel."

After we returned from dinner, he vomited continuously until dawn, at which point I called an ambulance. Tom, Audrey, and I waited with him in an uptown hospital hallway for hours.

A young doctor straight out of med school said Ryan could have a brain tumor. A more experienced doctor dismissed that gut punch, saying, "Vestibular neuronitis. In other words, one inner ear has suddenly failed for balance. Captain, this could be a career ender, as you can't even drive with this for at least three months, and you definitely will not fly in the next six months."

Ryan had good benefits and would be compensated for this time. My concern was his mental outlook. Ryan loved the experience of flying—not the airline company, not providing the service, but simply being in the clouds and talking to his friends, as he had told me years before.

When Ryan began his sick leave, Sarah phoned. She asked Ryan to attend a counseling session with her. He was happy to oblige. Once at the session, she asked him to write a check for a therapeutic facility in New Mexico to the tune of fourteen-thousand dollars. Sarah realized she had deep issues with relationships due to the abuse she had suffered as a child. She insisted her problems interfered with her life. It was a brutal reminder that her biological parents had rejected her, her foster parents had tortured her, and despite this, she had fared better than most who went through similar experiences. Ryan was willing to attend counseling with her, but he was in shock at her sudden check request in front of her therapist.

Ryan encouraged Sarah to continue counseling. During this time, I told my best friend, Earla, that my stepchildren were straining our marriage beyond its limits. I confided to my friend my frustrations with Adam's failed rehabs, Jacob's dropping out of college for rehab, and Sarah's demand for a rehab the likes of which we didn't even know existed. Earla tried to mediate between Defensive-Husband-in-Denial and Bare-Her-Soul-Wife.

As if to even the playing field, Ford had an underage drinking party at our home. All the rage Ryan had bottled up for Adam's and Jacob's drug use spewed out at the wrong target.

"You'll never amount to anything but a loser druggie on the street!" he raged at Ford.

Though his apologies followed, thoughts of a divorce arose in me. We worked through this, our lowest point, with prayer, marriage counseling, and time. Ryan stopped scapegoating his anger at his own sons on Ford.

Unexpectedly, though negatively motivated, Ford became an overachiever. He got a job at our local hardware store. His grades began to soar. He attended Jessa's Vanderbilt graduation in Nashville with us. Ford even helped me prepare for Ryan's fiftieth birthday party with our closest friends. He made new friends with goals like his own: entrepreneurialism and world travel. He was accepted into his first choice of universities and would ace his college years with good grades. Ford was growing fast into his 6 foot, 4 inch height, strikingly handsome with a tall toned physique. He stood above the crowd literally and figuratively and grew into a son we were both very proud of.

Ryan realized we sorely needed another getaway, but he didn't suggest the usual. Ryan came home from a Sunday service, made a phone call, then announced he was going to Jamaica to get a roof up on a school, and guess who would be the head chef to the crew if interested?

"Chef? Why not a teacher or an artist?" I protested.

"Because you have always enjoyed cooking. I am going, and I want to eat your food!"

Thankfully, Ryan returned to work after seven months off. His remaining right inner ear had compensated for the failed left one. He had passed a functional balance test in order to return to the cockpit. However, he would not be up on a rooftop in a developing country without me nearby. If he wanted me to go along, I told him, coffee and a morning shower were my must-haves.

My charge would be feeding a crew of twelve three meals a day, as well as painting a dining room mural. I made shopping lists for meals and paint supplies. I filled a duffel bag with nonperishable foods. When we arrived in Jamaica, customs officers hastily seized a third of the food from my bag—no doubt for their own personal use, the mission leader later explained.

***

The road to Port Maria was long and dusty. We saw many bare-chested, dreadlocked Rastafarians languishing in oppressive heat amidst clustered shanties. Our bus driver stopped for a cow who was deciding which lane it wanted to be in. Palm-lined roads led to famous resorts—Sandals, Beaches, Couples. The same stunning turquoise waters lapped against hovels and raw sewage around the next cove. We saw the pervasive damage Hurricane Ivan had caused. Recovery from that storm, in fact, was our reason for being there. As we went through areas tourists never see, the effects of poverty worsened. I remembered the depressed Appalachian hills as having offered much more.

The ride went on for almost three hours into the night, yet what ran through my head was that the tired people beside us depended on me for a meal when we arrived. Thank God a shy Jamaican beauty would act as my helper. Local traffic increased in speed as the roads decreased in width with no guard rails or lane markings. The warm hospitality of the welcoming Christians of St. Mary's in Port Maria soon calmed my nervousness.

Sleeping at Banana Street in Port Maria was otherworldly. Giant black cicadas flew into the light over my top bunk, landing on my neck where they perched despite my shrieks. No screens in Jamaica, mon! This pink-spotted white lady was mosquito food for that entire week.

Lizards with bulging orange necks hopped in and out to visit, but they were pleasant compared to the dogs and roosters. As we faded into sleep each night, dogs howled at the moon for hours until the roosters took over like banshees between the barreling trucks with missing mufflers. My roommates snored while my sleep was evasive.

Somehow, God gave me the energy I required. Within two days, I painted an 8 by 8-foot mural of bamboo branches and lizards. No one expected to eat fresh cornbread, cookies, and cakes, but this head chef loves to bake. More challenging were the entrees. Feeling inspired, though, I mixed together lobster, shrimp, and scallops for Seafood Newburg after the mission charge took me to the local beach and introduced me to the native fishermen as they came ashore. A creative lasagna followed, where I replaced classic lasagna sheets with plain egg noodles and swapped in local goat cheese for the ricotta.

The men could not have been more appreciative. Ryan, along with six Atlantans and one Jamaican, comprised a team that replaced the roof of the Galena Primary School, which had previously accommodated four hundred students. The team stripped away truckloads of rotted, damaged materials in jungle humidity under a beating sun. They attached a roof in three days.

On the third day, as the men were working hard to finish, a line began forming behind trees. One hundred children in crisp blue uniforms quietly marched around to where the workers could see them. When all were in place, the last smiling child in each line of ten held up signs that read: "Thank You. You put our education first. You made us feel important. God bless You."

No speeches or songs. Just signs held high by beautiful children who could learn again. Ryan was among eight men who, I knew, were etched as heroes in these children's minds. And in mine. Both of us felt extremely fortunate and fulfilled to have had this mission trip experience. We appreciated our life together more, yet were able to see Christ's love exemplified in people loving one another in a simpler, less materialistic culture after a highly destructive hurricane.

***

We came home in time to celebrate Dad's eightieth birthday. Dad was feisty as ever and praised Ford, who had just been accepted into a prestigious business college. We also told Dad our family should expect to gain another son he could be quite proud of…a son named Jack.

Jack was making a name for himself in college football. He played in the East-West Shrine Bowl in San Francisco. We traveled with his parents and Jessa to cheer him on in the new year of 2005. Jack was assigned Barry Bonds' locker. As family, we were ushered to stellar seats to watch him play with skill on the winning team.

Ryan was the perfect tour guide in San Francisco, one who never gets lost because of an internal compass in his brain. We rode cable cars, watched sea lions, and ate chocolate at Ghirardelli Square. We took in Chinatown, Fisherman's Wharf, the Golden Gate Bridge, and Alcatraz. On display were people with many bizarre piercings and a man who had spray-painted himself metallic gold from head to toe in this wild and crazy city.

That April, Ryan was on a layover at a bar in Redondo Beach, California, and I was housecleaning. Both of us heard on ESPN when Jack was drafted into the NFL by the Buffalo Bills. Some say the NFL stands for "not for long," but Jack began five seasons as a second string, which meant he played less than the stars do with far less injury exposure. His first purchase with an impressive salary was an equally impressive diamond ring for Jessa. He proposed marriage at Niagara Falls after a horse and carriage ride. We had a wedding to plan.

Jack was bounced from the Bills to the Titans to the Redskins for two years, finally ending with the Panthers. He treated us to NFL games where my binoculars centered on Jack and I said prayers for his safety, as he was a battering ram for massive strongmen. He endured the strain on his nerves, his body, and his relationship with Jessa, ending with an NFL career of five years and enough experience to coach admiring high-school students for a lifetime.

Jack's parents were college sweethearts and exemplified an enduring marriage through many ups and downs, as with most relationships. Jessa had been through the pain of my divorces and would value loyalty and commitment in her marriage. Jack provided her with security, and even fleeting NFL fame through the early part of their union. She would sail a better course than I had. Yet my third marriage was going strong after eight years.

Ryan did not renew his season tickets to the Pirates. He had plenty to keep him busy in his life as a husband, father, *and* pilot. Occasionally we rode the trolley downtown for a Pirates game in the evening. At one of these games, a summer thunderstorm delayed the action for two hours. Ryan assured me we would catch the last trolley southbound. Sure enough, we stood on the platform after the game and found ourselves entering the trolley on the southbound tracks. Once seated, we were able to read the train stops ahead in neon red letters. In a few stops, we realized we hopped on the wrong last train. A flashback from my college days brought on a full-blown panic attack. I was aware of every hammer of my heartbeat.

As a college sophomore, the pressures of difficult courses and confusing relationships overwhelmed me one night with depression and homesickness. I called my mother to tell her I really needed to come home for a long weekend. Would she make the just-under-two-hour trip north to pick me up?

"You can't expect me to be your chauffeur," she had replied. "If you want to come home, use public transportation. Take a train to Trenton and figure it out from there."

She made it sound easy. It was not easy. The first ride took hours on a train with many stops, ending in an area of a crime-ridden city that even today is down in the heels and does not give off a safe vibe. The second ride was by bus with more stops, ending in Lambertville, New Jersey.

This was as close to any road to Warrington that I knew of. I had to call my mother on pay phones along the way to let her know how far she would have to drive to pick me up: fourteen miles.

When I placed my last call to her, she told me to start walking those many miles. A half hour after I began walking, she picked me up along the side of a busy road at sunset. Never having traveled by public transportation alone, this experience was terrifying and exhausting. I would not repeat the trip again, other than in my nightmares where I find myself still riding on a strange train or bus, lost. I would never have purposely put my children in the danger this posed.

So here I was, reliving that nightmare on a trolley. The end of the line was a mall station late at night. No car awaited us. Thank God for cell phones and for Jessa who lived with us for just one last month. We hurriedly walked to a restaurant's entrance awning where she found us ten minutes later and took us to our car, two miles away.

***

Fern continued her counseling sessions past her twentieth birthday. After another summer of working at the country club, we transported her back to college for band camp. Then we transported Ford to his university in the Midwest. I found myself sobbing before we left him at his high-rise dorm. My only son and my youngest had chosen to study the farthest away.

For the first time, Ryan and I lived alone in our home as empty nesters, quietly. Our marriage up to this point revolved primarily around the activities of our children. We looked forward to having more time with and for each other, to travel, to make new friends, and to find new activities to enjoy.

***

Because I was now a full-time substitute teacher, we got a referral from Jack's mom for her cleaning lady. By coincidence, we learned that this woman's daughter, Brittany, was Fern's summer work friend. The mother admitted her daughter might have a problem with alcohol. Fern gravitated toward such rebels. It turned out this girl was more than a rebel…she was a sociopath.

The following semester, Fern's smoking pot with her college boyfriend led to her failing two courses. Then her college dean called to inform us that Fern was found guilty of plagiarizing a paper. She would have to finish her degree at another college, commuting from home. We did not want her to follow in Adam's footsteps and drop out of college to go from one drug crisis to another. Images of what Fern's future could be flashed through my mind and my nightmares. To ensure her compliance with this plan, we asked Fern to resume counseling, though she was not at all pleased to be doing so. We saw no alternative.

My own therapy was to immerse myself in creative projects. As long as I was painting, acting, singing, or writing, time took on a Zen-like dimension and some peace entered my world.

I created an entire mosaic wall in our study from seashells and landscape pebbles. I painted a huge sunflower mural in our bathroom under a skylight. And I played the Wicked Witch of the West at a respected Pittsburgh-area theater, complete with a fire-shooting broom, green face and hands, and a trap door to melt through when the bucket of water was thrown. This was my calm before the brewing storm. I was under a grand delusion that once my children went off to college, they would be all grown up, and parenting would become a stroll down Easy Street.

CHAPTER SIXTEEN

Foul Ball

On Fern's twenty-first birthday, her grandparents gave her their very used car. They were preparing to move into a retirement community with only one car permitted. We took the car to our local mechanic and poured money into it before he could deem it safe. Fern needed this gift to commute from home to the local college.

Two weeks later, friends invited us to visit them in Chicago for the weekend. Fern was in charge of our house and our loyal shepherd, Rex. While we were away, Fern never answered her phone, and when we returned, Fern was nowhere to be found. Rex wanted to tell us. Our answering machine revealed she was overdrawn at her bank, and she had missed her counseling appointment.

When she came home a few days later, we discussed our expectations. She did not come home that night either, and she did not go to her classes. One month after turning twenty-one, Fern came to our front door and spoke with me.

"I'm not coming home, Mom," she said, fuming. "I'm twenty-one. I'm doing what I want to do."

"Where is this anger coming from, Fern?" I asked her. I could feel my heart racing. "And don't say you are not angry."

"You drug test me and make me go to counseling. All my friends say that is horrible."

I asked her what she thought was the appropriate response to handling an adult child living in your home who was using drugs.

"Just be upset, but don't take action like what you're doing," she offered matter-of-factly.

"Do you think you can divest yourself from your whole family?" I asked with trepidation.

"No, but I will live with Brittany and her mom," she barked at me, daring me to disagree.

"Do you think your friends may have gotten in the way of your goals?"

She ignored the question. "I have decided to take off this semester. I am going to the college now to withdraw."

"We hope you will pray over this decision, but just tell me, do you have a drug problem?"

She continued to deny having a problem, saying all she did was smoke. Before she walked out and slammed the door, she said, "I'll come back tomorrow for my things. I'll call first."

Ryan and I immediately canceled our parent loan within the deadline. We changed our garage door code, fearful of the influence Fern's friends had on her behavior. Weeks went by with no contact. She never withdrew from the university and accrued large debts because of not doing so.

Fern was not taking her thyroid meds. We learned that she had made ATM overdrafts of almost a thousand dollars. Fern did not care. Where was the daughter we knew? Amy gave me an address where we found Fern and asked her to bring Brittany over for dinner. When they visited, Brittany mumbled when she spoke, to the point that Fern joked about being her translator, in addition to her driver and her maid. We could not get an answer as to why Brittany did not drive. We were about to find out, via a phone call in October.

"Mom, Brittany took my car last night and totaled it," Fern told me with a trembling voice. "She is in the hospital with both legs crushed. She stole my keys from my purse and she was totally ripped. I told her not to take my car, but she did anyway."

Fern still would not come home or take my advice, so we obtained a police report, which stated that at 3:30 a.m. the driver went into the oncoming lane at excessive speed. Smelling of alcohol, she was combative with the police, charged with DUI, and had contraband in the car.

I called Fern and read the report to her with an appeal to leave these toxic people and come home.

But Fern replied, "I'm needed at Amy's house to nurse Brittany while Amy works."

"She totaled your car when she was drunk and on drugs, and you are nursing her?" I yelled. I gripped the kitchen counter in disbelief.

"I'll be home at Thanksgiving. We will talk then. Bye, Mom," she said, then hung up.

***

We never saw Fern at Thanksgiving, though Fern's college friend, Mel, phoned us. She spelled out that Fern was being controlled by an addict and gave us an address. After many knocks at the door, a man with hollowed cheeks, Coke-bottle glasses, and a limp appeared.

"We are Fern's parents, and we need to speak with her. We have been very worried."

"She ain't here. A friend named Donny came and got her an' took her ta Johnstown," he drawled, blocking the door with is thin body.

"We dunno whar the car is," he offered, narrowing his suspicious, bloodshot eyes.

"It's in the police report where the car is and it has been there for weeks." I educated him.

"PO-lice! That's why Fern wuz here. Yinz guys wanted her to git Britny in trouble!"

"No, in fact," I offered, feeling my cheeks flush with impatience, "We wanted Fern to tell the police that Brittany stole her car."

"Fern gave her the car whenever she damned wanted it," he retorted, then shut the door in our face.

Soon Ryan and I were listening to a strikingly similar country accent at a rural junkyard.

"Yep, she jest crunched up like cellophane. It's a wonder the driver ain't dead," I remember the junkyard owner saying. He went on, describing all the beer cans he'd found in the back seat and the plastic neon tubes that had also been in the car, smelling of weed.

"Bein' drunk probly saved 'er cuz she didn't know what was goin' on when she crashed."

My teeth chattered, viewing the wreck. If Fern had been in that car, she would have died.

We lugged home bags and boxes. From many clothes, I washed out dirt, mildew, broken glass, and the stench of alcohol. It took days to save her wardrobe, which apparently had been stored in her car, now the ruined gift from her grandparents. My constant prayer was for Fern to be saved as easily, washed clean and restored.

***

In December, we received the first of many calls from Donny, Fern's college friend from of all places, Johnstown, the city of the historically tragic flood I had researched for my book club.

Donny was a newlywed, an admitted schizophrenic, a bi-polar man who was depressed, and had conflicted feelings for Fern. As if this wasn't enough, he told me his meds often backfired when he drank.

Fern had called him about her captive situation playing nurse to Brittany, whereupon Donny felt compelled to whisk Fern away, middle of the night, white-knight style. Donny offered Fern a place to live in his basement and employed her as a salesclerk at the mall shop he managed. While this arrangement sounded doomed to fail, she was far from Brittany. These calls gave me hope that Fern was beginning her life anew with supportive friends. I hadn't yet learned that users hang with users and thus, toxic relationships form.

***

Though Fern's twenty-first year had been rough, it was prosperous for the rest of our family. In Miami, we witnessed Adam marry Michelle, age nineteen, on a cruise ship where she declared that she wanted babies right away. She must not have heard the recommendation to get a plant together, then a puppy, and then a fact check on how you're doing as a couple before even thinking of bringing in a living, breathing baby to your marriage.

Jessa and I began planning her June wedding while Jack was house-shopping. Sarah was finishing her master's in counseling as Jacob and Ford were earning their bachelor's degrees in well-respected universities.

My creative outlet that year was working with a local playwright active in Pittsburgh theater. He cast me as the lead in his new play, which premiered downtown at the Open Stage Theatre. I portrayed a childless woman who was in a doomed marriage, kind of like I was in real life before Jessa's birth. Soon after, I emceed and modeled for a designer fashion show on that stage. I was getting my feet wet in theatrical venues of the city's cultural center. And as usual, Ryan was my biggest supporter and fan, attending every performance when he was not flying.

Despite all these happy events, Fern worried me. She was a joy as a child and so very lovely now. Yet she was her father's child, too. His addictions had ruined his life. They led to his abandoning his family. They contributed to the death of a young woman who was riding on his motorcycle while he was inebriated. I pitied him but worried those addiction genes had passed on to our daughter. I mailed a letter to Fern telling her of my fears. She responded by asking me to cosign a credit card. We had learned our lesson earlier from dealing with Sarah. She went into debt on our joint credit card that she did not repay. The heart of my message was that Fern could return home if Johnstown was not working. Fern didn't know Donny had called to say that she was recently carried out of a bar, passed out over a friend's shoulder.

"Think she was slipped a drug," Donny had told me, "but she drinks Southern Comfort and smokes pot 'til she's blotto."

I told him Southern Comfort had been her dad's booze of choice.

"Oh yeah, he called her this week…cried a lot. Told her he realizes what he missed when he's with his step-kids and sent her a grand to cover his guilt trip. And she met a guy at a bar named Chad. He is crazy for her. She's spending all her time at the place he shares with his cousin. Tells me he got his cousin off drugs. Maybe he can help Fern."

***

Fern was in love with Chad, and before long she wanted us to meet him for lunch, in an attempt to assure us she was in a healthier relationship. Oddly, he looked more like her brother than her real brother—tall, thin, sharp nose, and sad eyes. Over our lunchtime conversation, we learned that his life was altered when his mom, sister, and stepdad were killed in a boating accident. That difficult time was followed by a relative cutting him out of his parents' will. He was a seasonal laborer; thus, he was unemployed during Johnstown's long, bleak winters.

"So, you helped your cousin to get off of drugs?" I asked him.

I was sure he hadn't expected my bringing up the issue of drugs.

"Oh yes. I am so against drug use!" he blurted, a little too earnestly.

This was what I had wanted to hear, but it was not the truth. Chad was an expert liar.

Beware the Ides of March. That is precisely when Donny's next crisis call came.

"We do not want Fern here. Chad is a crack addict, and he's giving Fern crack. She said she smoked it five times. We urged her to break up with him. After agreeing to, she stole away at midnight," he told me, in a rush. "She made a mold of her body in her bed out of her clothes. You should have seen the trouble she went to—it was a work of art! You need to get her out of Johnstown. This is straining my marriage, but I am concerned for our safety…and Fern's life!"

I could hear how distressed he was. He continued, telling me she'd been fired from her job. "She decided not to go to work," he added, "and never called in to her manager, so you can't blame him."

Jessa, Ryan, and I traveled to Johnstown to bring Fern home after first getting her clothes from Donny. We convinced the police to escort us to the house where Donny told us she lived. She refused to come with us. We wanted to just grab her and put her in the car. She looked gaunt and had dark circles under her eyes. The officer told us that where she'd been staying was a crack house. He also told us crack often leads to cardiac arrest and death with just a single use. Yet, if we took her into our car against her will, the police would have to arrest us for kidnapping. Seeing her sister like this, Jessa was as frightened as we were. She appealed to Fern to come home, away from my earshot.

But Fern said to all of us, "I'm not going anywhere. I smoke crack because I want to." She added that she smoked maybe two hits every three days.

"I am not addicted. There are people in Johnstown who love me as much as family."

"Fern," I pleaded with her, "if you believe people who give you crack love you, then you *are* in big trouble!"

At the urging of the police, Ryan and I went to a Parents of Teenage Alcohol and Drug Abusers (POTADA) meeting where parents shared their heartache resulting from their children's addictions. "Let Go and Let God," was their motto.

Fern was not a minor, so our options were nil. Ford came up with the idea that we both email Jon. He thought that as Fern's father and as an addict himself, he might be able to reach out to her effectively. I first emailed saying he had the chance to save his daughter's life by getting her out of a crack house and in so doing, he might feel better about himself. His response? Calling me not only a "pompous-ass bitch," but a "controlling bitch," adding that if Fern was having problems, it was from me raising her.

Then Ford defended me in this email:

"Mom's raising of Fern has nothing to do with her addictions and poor decisions. She raised her with Christian morals and taught her to be a lady. Jessa and I live our lives making wise decisions and living ethically. Being your youngest, I only know you from what I've been told. You're an alcoholic, having narrowly escaped death and jail. You left Mom with nothing while she raised kids you state you love twice a year in a card. I don't know how your relationship was with your dad, but stand in my shoes. When I have a family, I'll deal with fatherhood better than you. Fern needs an intervention away from other addicts. It hurts me, but it hurts Mom more. She's a generous, caring mother who is trying to protect Fern. Fern's weakened emotional psyche has killed any possibilities for an easy life, which my parents gave her every opportunity to earn. An intro biology class would show your addictive genes passed down to her. It's nature, not nurture. Some shit you can't control."

What a powerful treatise from the son of an alcoholic to the dad who abandoned his children. I'd never again contact Jon. He dashed his one chance to help his child. At the same time, I could not have been prouder of my son for defending me and seeing this crisis so clearly.

Surprisingly, Fern reached out to Jack in the summer of 2008, admitting she needed help but saying that Chad was worse off. Yet she would not leave him. Even her college roommate, Mel, visited Fern to ask why she was living there. Fern told her it was so she could save Chad. Mel was aghast at Fern's burnt fingers and needle-tracked arms. She begged Fern to live with her for a while because she looked incredibly haggard. Fern told her she could visit only if Chad said it was okay, declining Mel's lifeline.

The next day the police issued a search warrant for the crack house. Chad and Fern were evicted. Fern asked Donny to drive her to Mel's house, from where our family could get her into treatment. We all held our breath. If this plan of Donny and Mel's worked out, she would be away from Johnstown's drug culture for good.

Then Donny called to tell me that Fern had jumped out of his car and hitched a ride back to Chad. "Can you call Mel and tell her not to expect us?"

This call devastated me. We began to plan an intervention. Everyone would read a letter they wrote to Fern with a counselor mediating. We knew Fern was going to make an effort to be at Jessa's wedding shower when we all would be there to do this, but Jessa and Jack were against it. Dad said he was bringing a gun to "scare the shit out of Chad." Are guns at interventions the standard operating procedure?

Jessa and Jack went to Johnstown to bring her to the shower. Jessa pleaded to me to put off the intervention.

"Fern wants to be in the wedding. She won't mess up," she said. "We saw Chad. That weasel slunk away after telling us he's picking her up tomorrow. They're brain-fried by drugs."

The bridal shower went well. Fern was helpful, even sociable. Our phone bill revealed she made twenty calls to Chad within twenty-four hours. He got lost repeatedly, taking four hours to drive a two-hour trip. He called when he was finally nearby.

A twenty lay on the kitchen counter where we were standing. Fern eyed the bill. I snatched it up. She began to physically attack me for the money.

"What in *hell* are you doing, Fern? Stop it!" Jessa yelled as she pried her sister off me.

Fern told us Chad would not come in to listen to our—I believe the word was "shit."

Now Jessa was in charge. "Really? *I'm* going to go outside and tell him he *will* come in!"

What followed was not a family intervention but rather a family confrontation in our living room after Chad slunk in. He really did resemble a weasel in his gait, sly looks, and snarly mouth.

"Chad, it is hard for us to trust you with Fern since you lied to us about your drug use from the get-go."

"Man, this whole thing has been blown way out of proportion," he protested.

"Let me ask you one question. Would your mom want you to be using drugs?" I asked.

"No, she wouldn't, but it's not like we're addicted or anything. We just do it when we want to."

Then, he added, "Fern asked me for it. She wanted it. So yeah, I gave it to her."

What a guy, I thought.

Jessa and Ryan sat on either side of me, silently giving me strength. I took a much-needed slow breath before I continued. Fern's arms were crossed tightly. Her angry glare was piercing.

"Let's say you're with friends. They offer you crack. Do you take it?" I said.

"Well yeah, if it's there, and they ask us to take some, we'll, like, take it," Chad said.

"But you don't believe you have an addiction or need professional help?" I asked.

It was apparent their denial was the Great Wall of China that I was slamming against.

"Oh man, like this is really hard to talk about," Chad sighed. "I don't, like, need crack or have a problem."

"Are you aware that crack can kill you from just one dose? Have you ever read about it?"

"Oh my God! Crack does not kill you. Why are you saying this to us?" he asked me.

I was the crazy one. They announced they were leaving and didn't want to talk anymore.

***

Thank God for POTADA meetings. We were not the only parents facing this insanity. And thank God for a husband who flew me to beautiful places to ease the madness. We went to St. Kitts on a free Marriott time-share vacation. We declined the investment but enjoyed seeing the wild pigs, monkeys, and mongoose living there. We visited some fun friends in southern California to tour the serenity of San Juan Capistrano together. We visited Ford in Indiana and enjoyed hearing of his first hilarious experiences at the Indy 500, where he pretended that he was a gay Austrian around redneck spectators. His comedy routine had his friends in stitches, as well as his parents.

And oh, how we needed to laugh.

CHAPTER SEVENTEEN
Season Opener

Spring is a time for new life. We learned Adam and Danielle were expecting twin boys, making us first-time grandparents. Delighted, we gave them money toward their first home. Conversely, we were shocked to hear Fern's news over the phone—of her pregnancy. She *said* she was staying clean but had been on drugs at the time of conception. She had broken up with Chad and would raise the baby alone. Fern's life was not healthy or stable. Add a baby to this?

I asked my gynecologist for his opinion on the health of this baby. His outlook was grim. Later, I told Fern, "If you have this baby, it will not be healthy and Chad will *always* be in your life."

"I cannot have an abortion because that would cost thousands of dollars, Mom."

"Fern, we will support whatever decision you make, but please give this a lot of thought."

Days later I wrote a check for far less than Fern thought she would need. The hardest moments came at the entrance to Planned Parenthood. There a protester screamed at us, "Do not go in there! That could be your beautiful grandchild!"

I wanted to scream back, "Have you experienced a child born with birth defects due to a drug? Have you seen your firstborn hooked to machines, in pain with every breath? Have you had folks ask how your baby is, having just buried her in a small white coffin? Have you worked as a professional advocate for children with severe disabilities? Have you seen children born to mothers on drugs who would be completely dependent on them every minute of their lives? Do you know the millions of dollars, tears, and sleepless nights it takes for their care? Did you raise children as a single mom, barely paying the bills, grateful for your WIC coupons to get you by? Have you seen the pain in your son's eyes when it is Dad's Night in first grade and his alcoholic dad has long ago abandoned him? Is your child afflicted with addiction genes? Have you seen her give up her education, her family, her health—all for the next rush? Have you seen her once-beautiful face, now with sunken eyes and discolored teeth, viewing you as her enemy? Will her disabled, heroin-addicted baby be easily placed into an adoptive home? I am guessing all of your answers to my questions are *no*!"

I felt pure rage at their judgment of our mere presence there that day. These sick crazies hold up grotesque signs of aborted tissue that children and old ladies see as they pass. They have no compassion for people like Fern and me and what we have endured. Are their worlds so twisted that they purposely inflict guilt on others on one of the worst days of their lives? "Judge not, lest you be judged" is what they certainly do *not* live by.

We made our way past them.

It was as if I was in the same room from thirty years ago when I sat by Sharon, but this time I was holding my daughter's trembling hand, listening to the same suctioning sound.

"This may sound crazy, but listen to your mom," a nurse said afterward to Fern, feeling our deep grief. "She loves you. I wish I'd listened to mine. Now let's talk about aftercare."

I visited Fern in her new apartment in Johnstown ten days later with food and supplies. She swore Chad was out of her life. She had a new job at a sign shop she walked to. She was looking forward to coming to the wedding. That day I delivered her plane tickets to do just that.

***

My mother visited me, unaware of all this drama that had been centering around Fern.

"What a beautiful spring day! I brought some fruit for you!" she greeted me.

As Mom handed me the bag, she saw I was taken off guard by the weight of it.

"Oh, it's just your father's World War II pistol, and ammunition magazines are in there, too."

"With the fruit? And just what do I want with Pop's gun?" I asked her incredulously.

"Your father is acting crazy again. He says if he cannot kill Chad at an intervention, he will do it at the wedding. Pop is sure he will show up there. You hold onto it for me," she said.

"Pop's gun will be locked up. But Fern has made it clear that Chad is not coming to the wedding."

"Pop's eighty-three. He says, 'What are the cops gonna give me? Life?' Keep it for me!"

***

Fern was her sister's maid of honor on that June wedding day. She looked gorgeous standing at the altar beside graceful, joyful Jessa. Fern blended in seamlessly, and many guests commented on how lovely all of my children were. We were blessed that day with hope for the future.

Fern was clearly nervous as she rose to toast her sister and Jack. What followed was the most honest and heartfelt toast I have ever heard. The love she felt for both of them radiated.

"Ever since I can remember, I looked up to Jessa," Fern began. "She looked out for Ford and me. We called her our second mom. She knew how to pick a good guy. Upon meeting Jack, it was obvious he was in love with her, as he couldn't keep his eyes off of her."

She continued: "We grew closer recently when I went through a rough time. He was there for me. My prayer someday is to find someone with as big a heart, as good a head on his shoulders as Jack. Here's to your happiness."

Ryan and I took to the dance floor and felt terrific, having taken lessons and having lost weight in anticipation of this celebration. We rediscovered our love for each other at the wedding. We were days from celebrating ten years since our engagement at that Pirates game.

On our anniversary, we reminisced at the ball park, but this time we sat at the club level drinking wine. Then we went to the Hyeholde Restaurant, where we had our first date. And yes, we sat at our special table, and I still got into that same red dress. My husband was as romantic as I could have wished for. We loved each other, and we loved our life in the city of Pittsburgh.

CHAPTER EIGHTEEN

Safe at Home Plate

Fern's new job at the sign shop did not last long, and neither did her stay in her new apartment. Perhaps that was due in part to her reuniting with Chad. She was back to saving him. This prompted our decision to stop paying on her college loans. Ryan sent her our intervention letters, along with the college loan coupons in her name. We told her that if she ever returned to college, we would assist her again. I longed for my once-motivated beauty, my affectionate hugger and jokester.

At the end of the summer, we got a call from her landlord saying she had been evicted. Mom's childhood bed was left behind, among other possessions. We paid her back rent to get them. Fern showed up just before we arrived, but when the landlord advised her that we were coming, "She took off a-runnin'," he said.

Ford was with us. Fern didn't even want to see her brother.

The landlord told us, "She's got a no-good boyfriend. His money goes straight to drugs. An empty bottle of Suboxone was found in the bathroom. It's for gettin' off heroin."

"Mom, I am disgusted with her!" Ford said. "You have to divorce her just like she is doing to us. She may not come home for ten years, and you cannot put yourself through this anymore!"

Ford knew I'd escaped pain via divorce. It seemed a simple solution to him. He just didn't realize a mother can't divorce her child. He just wanted to ease my hurt. It was time to attend to my other children, who had understandably run out of patience with a wayward sister.

***

The newlyweds returned from their idyllic Kauai honeymoon, so we flew to see Jack play in his first Titans game. We gained access to private areas to see the players, and we were treated at a steakhouse overseen by Jack's dad. Jessa was about to begin her dream job as a pediatric nurse practitioner. She was overjoyed to begin her married life in the city where they shared college memories and where her new husband now played in the National Football League. It was a needed break for us to see these two newlyweds, whom we so loved, at the peak of their happiness and success.

***

In 2007, Ryan was privileged to fly a chartered flight that carried 146 veterans to our nation's capital to see the newly erected World War II monument. After the trip, during lunch, he was telling me all about it. Then, from the radio, we heard the lead story: "The airline company announced the closing of the PIT pilot base effective January first."

We were shocked.

"Five years from retirement, and we are faced with moving!" Ryan cried out.

We had met in Pittsburgh, a city we both knew and loved. We had raised our kids there for the excellent school system. My parents were only a few miles away. This would be a huge change—new friends, new town, new climate, new culture. We were overwhelmed.

And then I thought of Fern, who had not contacted us in months. Pittsburgh would no longer be her home base. We were forced to call Donny. He said he would get word to her to call me. When she did, she blamed her last eviction on me and told me not to come to visit until they found a better place to live. We attended POTADA meetings more frequently, while we still could.

***

Ford was preparing to study at Reutlingen University in Germany for a semester abroad.

"Reutlingen! Does Ford realize he has relatives in that city?" Mom asked, after I shared this news with her. "My ninety-nine-year-old great aunt and her family live there. I'll give my cousins a call! They'll be thrilled."

We visited Ford in Reutlingen. By then, my relatives there were offering him a welcoming second home. We had previously met their teenage daughter, Silke, when she had visited America years earlier. These folks were kin to a grandpa I never knew because of divorce, yet I credit my artist genes to that grandfather, a mural artist by trade. We met my grandfather's sister. She was surprisingly spry, and appeared to be an elderly version of her niece, my mother. We stayed for three days at the home of Silke's parents. They did not speak a word of English. Somehow, I resurrected basic German from the depths of my brain.

They spoiled us with huge meat-filled German meals in a home crafted of hardwoods. Aromas from my grandma's kitchen filled the air: dark crusty bread, plump boiled knockwurst, and vinegary potato salad. They showed us where my great-grandparents lay buried in their backyard orchard.

I strolled through the ancient cathedral nearby where my ancestors were baptized and buried, and I felt a connection to my German heritage.

Best of all, I saw Ford, now bilingual and loving his European sightseeing with new friends. He was thriving in business classes taught in German and began a minor in the language. He returned home just before Christmas, a handsome young man, now bitten badly by the travel bug. We were shown such wonderful hospitality from relatives we just met. As Ford was now earning straight A's, he effortlessly landed a summer internship in Chicago upon his return.

***

When we returned home, Adam and Michelle's twins were born, prematurely. Ryan flew to Tampa, where the babies were transported and in incubators. Though perfect to look at, it would be months before we knew the ramifications of their premature birth. I, of all people, knew firsthand the strain that a tragedy involving babies puts on a marriage. I'd never seen babies this tiny. I had vast experience with the developmental disabilities that accompany premature births.

We visited the new family months later and stayed with Jacob. He was renting one of his mother's rental homes. We attended his long-anticipated college graduation, where he earned a degree in communications. We had lunch with Ryan's ex-wife, where conviviality was stilted.

In Jacob's kitchen, prominently displayed, was a lab slip tacked to a cork board. Under "diagnosis" it said, "unspecified immune disease," and it listed titer levels for Jacob. I asked my own doctor about this after a preliminary search on the internet. My suspicions were confirmed that this was the test used to monitor HIV. Jacob told us he needed a job with full insurance coverage. Ryan made no queries.

"If he wanted me to know of HIV, he would have told me," Ryan predictably responded.

***

Though we didn't want to move, there was a short timeline for the company to pay for it. There was no use fighting the inevitable. As my mother used to say, life was handing us lemons and we should make lemonade. We were not fond of the weather in Pittsburgh, so there was at least one reason to be glad to leave.

We started house hunting. We chose to live by a lake close to the airport. Since Ryan's family lived in the Carolinas, we had selected the Queen City as his work base. The only people we knew in the area were sister-in-law Audrey and her husband, Tom, but they lived on the opposite end from the airport, too far away for us to consider.

We flew south, rented a car, and began to browse neighborhoods. We stopped into a realtor's office and met Deb and Jill from New Jersey. They gave us more information than we could digest and were charming and really, truly kind. We could not get serious until we sold our home, but we set our budget and must-have lists.

We prepared our home for sale. We stripped wallpaper, moved clutter into storage, and shipped boxes to our children. We gathered a carful of Fern's possessions, but she did not return messages or answer letters. No matter what, they would not be tossed, as my mother had done with my possessions back in Warrington. That had felt like a part of my life had been erased, discarded, and it had hurt deeply. Despite the pain Fern's actions had caused, her material treasures were not mine to throw away.

***

I badly needed a hysterectomy due to fibroid tumors, and I did not want to deal with a new doctor in a strange hospital to undergo this surgery. January found me with thirteen staples across my lower belly. Ryan was my loving nurse, assisting my quick healing.

With plenty of time in bed, I wrote my first full-length play about Fern. The words poured out easily. I needed to find some order through our experienced chaos.

The Pittsburgh Playwrights Theatre Company held a playwright competition. The winners would get to stage their plays downtown. The next month, I directed a staged reading of my play there with supportive friends in the cast. Members of our POTADA support group attended and empathized with my need for this creative outlet.

My last foray into local theater was directing my favorite musical, *Man of La Mancha*. I was paid amply and knew the talented folks at the regional theater well. Aside from casting a spoiled, overweight, know-it-all diva as Dulcinea, it was a memorable show with full houses.

***

In the spring, Ryan went into atrial fibrillation, with chronic irregular rate and rhythm of his heartbeat. After being admitted to the hospital, he was released with instructions to take medication. When the condition persisted, he went back into the hospital for monitoring. This all occurred within a forty-eight-hour period. Ryan put on a false front of normalcy when his health went awry…while I panicked. Eventually, his brother, brother-in-law, father, and mother would all come down with the same condition. My assumption is that an irregular heartbeat is normal for this family.

Of course, Ryan now couldn't fly due to the rigid FAA regulations, and his medical team told him he needed periodic stress tests and close follow-up if he wanted to return to the cockpit. We did not know then that this would be a lifelong condition. We soon realized the perfect timing of this malady, however. Ryan had the time to join me in house shopping, as well as in helping to get our home ready for sale. We put the house on the market in the beginning of May, and within four weeks we had an excellent offer. My parents said we would never get our price, but we did in no time. We purchased a new home, Ryan's favorite listing, just down a country lane from a lake, in the very same town where we had last seen my first husband in family court years ago.

Before moving, we got a call from Fern's former endocrinologist. Fern had sent disability forms, wanting the doctor to say Fern was due social security disability payouts. Of course, the doctor refused. With daily medication, there is absolutely no reason a person with hypothyroidism cannot work. No doubt her friends on government assistance prompted this attempt to scam the system.

The phone call motivated us to make a surprise visit to Fern. On Father's Day, we loaded our car with all of her possessions, and we surprised her and Chad at their door. We had no choice, as we could not move the contents of her old room with us. Tears fell when I first saw her living so poorly with her Mr. Wrong.

I carry few memories of this visit other than a haze of depression knowing we would be much farther away from each other. But the miles did not cause the division. It was the drugs and the wrong peers. A memory of Wolf's favorite saying to his juvenile court-appointed clients came to me: "If you hang with wolves, you'll howl like one." How ironic, with his first name.

We took photos of Ford standing in front of the house in which he had spent half of his life. We said goodbye to our clubs, choir, support group, theater friends, neighbors, and, of course, to my parents, who cried at this unexpected change in all our lives. We never wanted to leave Pittsburgh, but an airline company had forced our hand. Movers packed up all of our worldly goods into a moving truck, and we spent our last day in our modest, suburban brick house, which had been a cozy home to four of our children. We had moved so many times by now that I viewed any move as an enema for our life, where we flush out all the excess "stuff."

On the first day of summer, we arrived at my sister-in-law's home in Charlotte with our loyal companion, Rex, and, as we would soon hear many times, it was hotter than blue blazes!

CHAPTER NINETEEN
Force Play

Our immediate concern when moving to the deep south was our beloved dog, Rex. He loved his treed yard with the invisible fence in the northern climate of suburban Pittsburgh. Here, he was in a new home with high humidity under the beating southern sun. At least the wildlife amused him. Red foxes crept about at dusk. Shy white-tailed deer leaped, and on rare occasions mangy coyotes slunk through our modest backyard. Rex soon adjusted to his two walks a day, a third of a mile, down to a charming community park with tall shade trees.

There by the boardwalk along the lake shore, he chased Canada geese into sparkling waters, or he stood at my side as people reeled in channel catfish. Once Ryan texted me, "Look up!" The Airbus he was piloting appeared above the tree line. Rex pranced in circles at my arm-waving excitement.

We wanted to find a church. Prayer, choir, and worship were the glue in our marriage. We had learned by now that we could not get through what life throws at us without the assistance of our personal Lord. We knew no one here and a shared faith is one way to make new friends.

We visited one in the town center. The minister was friendly, yet it was Harry who made us feel most welcome. His soft, gentlemanly drawl was reminiscent of Ashley Wilkes in *Gone with the Wind*.

"Ahr ya'll neuw ta our church? What brings ya'll heah?" Harry asked politely.

"I'm an airplane pilot. My wife's an actress and artist," quiet Ryan said, surprising me.

What we did not know was that Harry was the city's benefactor of the arts, having *given* the downtown art gallery to the town. His eyes lit up.

"Ahm gonna have a playwright call y'all tamahrah," he said before leaving us.

We soon got a call from a stranger.

"Ah'm Tommy an' Ah'd like ta invite ya'll ta mah studio tamahrah," he said, with an equally pronounced drawl.

Tommy gave me a tour and welcomed me as a member of his playwright group, teaching me much about writing one-act plays. I wore many hats as actress, director, and playwright with his small company. It was a black-box, no-frills studio theater in a warehouse on the edge of town. Tommy introduced me to Greg, a playwright, journalist, and former professor. We directed each other's plays to get our collaboration going. Greg became the bright, funny brother I never had. We meshed on a creative level and would forever work together in dinner theaters, plays, and movies. Greg lived with his sweet mother, an artist who also encouraged and inspired me. All of these new friends cascaded down from meeting Harry. Harry introduced Ryan to the gifted choir director Mary Ann. She welcomed us into her choir and into her circle of witty, fascinating friends. We found a church where we felt we belonged for a time, all thanks to hospitable Harry.

***

That summer brought news of Adam and his wife splitting up. The strain of his addiction cycles, while caring for physically challenged twins, took its toll, predictably. They lost the home our down payment helped them to purchase. The failed national economy contributed to this. Adam had not held lucrative, steady jobs, yet Jacob took the chance of renting a condo with his older brother. And most tragic of all, the family had been hit around this time with the results of the twins' MRIs: cerebral palsy. These angelic, alert, brown-eyed toddlers would never walk on their own.

***

That fall, a neighbor said when she heard of my theater and teaching background that I should apply to the local university. Tommy told me to do the same. My resumé found its way to the chair of the theater department. To my surprise, he phoned me a few days later, offering me a job. Would I teach four acting classes and one in theater history? An instructor position was suddenly open and the department chair was desperate to fill the slot. I accepted the job with the hope of meeting other theater professionals while teaching a favorite subject. The challenging part was learning the computer system and creating syllabus in three days. My computer level is preschool, much to Ford's frustration. Yet, the new boss assured me, "As long as the students give you good ratings, I promise you will have a job here."

And what a cool job it was! My students were engaging, polite, and creative. The meager salary I received did not measure up to the joy of teaching an art form that helps with posture, public speaking, interviewing, storytelling, and becoming a more creative and entertaining person. I cast one of my best students in a play I directed at Tommy's theater. Students earned extra credit to attend and review the play. For many, it was their first theater experience other than church skits.

***

Our weekends were spent enjoying the nearby lake. We did not want the expense of a boat, so we bought kayaks. On Thanksgiving, Ford and I paddled past mansions on mirror-smooth water. We explored coves, surprising yellow-bellied turtles, blue herons, and jumping largemouth bass. Ford went shooting with Ryan after he received his concealed-carry permit. These were opportunities we never explored up north. A neighbor invited us to a welcome party for new families in the neighborhood. Hospitality and wine flowed. The south was growing on us.

My parents visited us to sample a week of our first southern autumn. It was the last time Dad would have the strength to go fishing, and thankfully he caught a few. Ryan and I showed my parents around our small city and the university. Neighbors gave us a tour of the lake by boat. We watched Jack play in an NFL game on television.

Mom commented, "Southern restaurants are not for me. They plop a big bowl of bitter collard greens down in the middle of the table." I didn't want to call her out on this at the time, but I am still waiting for someone to bring me that bowl, in any Southern restaurant, even once.

***

Ryan was back to flying after seven months of medical leave due to his chronic atrial fibrillation. I loved having him home, but as always, he was eager to get back in the cockpit. In any other profession, he would have returned in seven days, but the FAA had him jump through hoops of testing and consulting with physicians. And when he finally got his clearance, we flew to the Big Apple for a day to see the uplifting musical *Mama Mia!* in celebration.

When I returned to my job, there was a note to see my boss, who robotically announced, "You will not be teaching in January due to budget cuts." He had not expected my tears. Obama had just won the election on "Change you can believe in." This change sucked.

My locally famous artist friend told me to send an email to the college president. It was my undoing. My student evaluations were glowing. I became convinced that my job cut was part of some political game because the next opening in the department was filled by a current professor's wife who had no graduate degree. The security of my job had not actually been about my stellar student reviews, as was promised. Yet my disappointment quickly ebbed when some unique artistic opportunities came my way unexpectedly.

CHAPTER TWENTY
Major League Player

Through a theater endeavor, I was about to gain another chosen brother. Whenever I heard of friends who had brothers they adored, I felt like I had missed out. I bonded easily with Mike and while we attended the same church for many years, we were very close. And it all began over a church pageant. Someone placed me on the casting committee. It was a job comprised of paperwork and random begging to fill roles. "Want to be a wise man? Sign here." This is against everything I had learned about casting. A man watched my unease at the table.

"Mah name's Mike an' Ah'd luv yer hayelp," he said in one of the thickest southern accents that I had ever heard. "We have a project known as The Last Supper drama an' we need a directah."

"Do you really *mean* director?" I asked, with much doubt.

"Trust me. We'll give ya' free creyaytive reign," he said with hopefulness in his eyes.

I rewrote the script, cast the roles in my own way, and the performance took place Maundy Thursday. This endeavor became my faith walk over the next eleven years. The audience saw the disciples portrayed as ordinary men who had extraordinary callings. I became an honorary brother, with a token coin and a pink bible to prove it, of the thirteen men in my cast. Mike became my chosen brother and trusted friend by handing me this directorial role.

***

Ford graduated college early, just like his eldest sister. Jessa flew with us to his graduation, and we took him and his friends out to lunch. We met Kaylyn. His friends warned us he had fallen hard and fast. His first words about her to me were, "Mom, she's a girl way out of my league."

She looked like Olivia Hussey from Zeffirelli's *Romeo and Juliet*, petite and with a long mane of curly hair. For his first big date, he confided to me, "Mom, I promised to show her France and Spain. Can I have a buddy pass?"

"Ford, you've set the bar too high," I told him, in reference to this flying perk of deeply discounted seats we had because of Ryan. "What's wrong with Burger King and a movie?"

Out of my love for him, though, that buddy pass would soon materialize.

***

Our year ended in Pittsburgh at the home of Jack's parents. Fern and Chad made the trip. Pop was there and did not murder Chad after all. He did make Fern cry, however, when he turned to Chad and decreed, "You have got to go to a trade school and learn a trade, rather than remain a laborer." She felt that her grandfather was demeaning her true love by suggesting a better path.

This was good advice. But by now we had all realized Chad was not the cause of Fern's problems. Fern was. By now it was clear Fern had inherited her father's addictive personality. Then Wolf's alcoholism had been on full display to this impressionable young girl. Life with Ryan had come a little too late to serve as a positive influence on Fern.

***

The new year began with an exotic vacation. We flew to Los Angeles and then to Tahiti to board a three-masted ship that held only one hundred passengers. The king and queen of Sweden were to be on this cruise with their aristocratic friends but cancelled at the last minute. We bunked in the cabin that had been set aside for their bodyguards, next to the owner's suite. We snorkeled in coral gardens with baronesses, sharks, and sting rays. We packed our old Windjammer pirate and prostitute costumes on a whim. Each night, dinner had a different theme. Upon hearing it was Nautical Night, we knew we had to bring some fun into this rather stodgy group of aristocracy.

A distinguished friend of the king came up to our table when he noticed our costumes.

"My name is Beau. I must get to know you two," said a genial elderly man.

We learned that two of his babies had died of birth defects; thus, he began a foundation providing folic acid for pregnant mothers worldwide. He asked the occasion for our trip. We produced a photo of Ford graduating from college and said he was the youngest of our six. Beau recognized the Indiana University logo and blurted, "I'm a Hoosier! I went to IU! People were kind to me there! I want to pay it forward to your son!" Heaven smiled upon Ford on that day.

That spring, Beau treated Ford and Kaylyn to dinner in a castle on the French Riviera on the promised travel pass. Ford received an internship with the global company Beau founded, a vital stepping stone in his career. This was our reward for dressing up as a pirate and prostitute in the middle of the sea. It also earned us a seat at the captain's table on the last night of the cruise, as well as a round of drinks from the owner of the cruise line. Did we dress for success? Yes!

Ford waited until he was eligible for in-state tuition to begin graduate school. He majored in IT and international business and was hired by a world-renowned accounting firm before graduation. Ford was on his way to a stellar future with his formal education behind him. Next, he would learn the intricate politics of real-world businesses.

***

Fern called us while we were away and told us of the death of Chad's father. In his forties and newly remarried with a baby, he succumbed quickly to liver cancer. Tragedy had taken nearly every member of Chad's immediate family. We visited Fern and Chad in the spring. They moved to an old house in a safer part of town that had been converted into apartments. They owned no dining table and stood on a stained carpet that resembled a bad tie-dye pattern. Fern often spent time with Chad's nieces, despite their mother's obvious annoyance when she did.

This same mother was scamming her social worker for government assistance by lying and saying that the father of her children had abandoned them. In reality she would tell him to go away for the day when the social worker scheduled a visit. My heart ached at Fern's choice to replace our family with Chad's, but thankfully, there was exciting family news about to come.

"Want to guess what NFL team I'll be on?" Jack asked on my next birthday. "It's the Carolina Panthers. Can I come live with you?"

He already knew my answer. We screamed with delight. Four months of bonding with Jack ensued. We spent our days around the pool memorizing *my* lines from theater roles and *his* football callouts, playing center. Jessa said her husband often felt more at ease with me than with his own mother. I was glad he felt this way, as my parents never saw the good in any of my husbands who were on their best behavior around their in-laws, ever critical of them.

At practice Jack suffered a severe concussion. His coach told him to go home to rest with no concussion protocol. Only the big stars were pampered. Sadly, many ex-players never know the results of chronic traumatic encephalopathy until years later. This was expertly documented in the 2015 movie *Concussion*. Once again, all I could do to handle this fear was to pray for Jack.

My friend Mike was in charge of the men's group and organized a church trip to the Panther Camp, where Jack promised to get a team-autographed football for our church auction. The Panthers were going to have the best fan they ever had: me.

Jack's parents visited us. We went to the last pre-game, against the Pittsburgh Steelers, in 2009. Jack played well, and was cut…and someone stole the promised autographed football from his locker that night. Ryan has a saying about the UNC Tarheels: "ABC," or Anybody but Carolina. It is my saying now. Now, I root against the Panthers every year—the mother-in-law curse—and it has worked well. Ever wonder why they lost the 2016 Superbowl to the Broncos?

***

I joined the church choir, where Ryan was already a valued bass. After choir rehearsals on Wednesdays, seven couples met for drinks and plenty of laughter. Because it was the second part of Wednesday nights, we were "W-2." These choir members became our closest friends, as we socialized with them and sang with them twice each week over the next decade.

They are funny, caring, bright peers who make any excuse to have a party. The first party in our new home was to celebrate the recovery from a mastectomy for Jane, my alto friend. For many years we had monthly girl parties out, celebrating our birthdays and friendship.

The constancy of these supportive friendships has been therapeutic in the mutual bonding and trust we have established. Through birth, death, marriage, divorce, illness, and recovery these group members are there for one another. There is power in a circle of women who pray with and for one another, a fact that has been known since ancient times.

CHAPTER TWENTY-ONE
Herky-Jerky Motion

On Fern's twenty-fourth birthday, I left a telephone message, but she did not return the call. I contacted Chad's employer and asked to leave a message for Chad or Fern to call her parents. Only then did she return my call, quite angry that she was found in this way. This was a continuation of Fern's disinterest in contacting her family for months at a time. To assuage her anger, we extended an invitation to her and Chad for a family Christmas with us using our travel passes. Surprisingly, Fern and Chad did join us in our home, along with Ford, Jessa, and Jack. Chad had nothing in common with the others, yet despite this strain, everyone was welcomed with presents under the tree and lots of home-cooked food. My persistence paid off to get Fern back into the fold. I was never about to disown her or give up on her, despite her addictions.

***

We returned to Pittsburgh to celebrate New Year's Eve at a party with my parents in their retirement community. The north's biting winds were jolting. Living in the Land of

Cotton had spoiled us, but we were planning an escape to Caribbean waters to avoid the gray of winter.

Windjammer Cruises went out of business due to mismanagement by the founder's heirs. We sampled a new company that was hoping to win over the old customers and flew to Grenada to sail on the *Diamante*. Only six couples could book on this much smaller ship, and we all got seasick as the waves rocked her. In fact, Ryan did a backward flip down the aft steps when the tiny ship rolled. He was unhurt, probably thanks to the effects of the complimentary island rum.

Snorkeling with sea turtles off a tiny cay where larger ships were unable to navigate and having the best lobster pizza of our lives on the island of Bequia made up for the rough seas.

When the cruise ended, we were delayed in Barbados for a night. Planes were downsized, paying passengers were accommodated, and hitchhikers like us were left high and dry, scrambling to come up with alternative plans. There were much worse places to be stuck as we sipped island drinks under a tiki roof on a pristine beach at sunset. This was the adventurous part of being a pilot's wife that made up for his forever working holidays and weekends. No, pilots don't work just on weekdays, and only the company's most senior pilots get to take the holidays off.

It was hard to get Ryan relaxed enough to open up about his adult children. Walks on tropical beaches were a good place to start. Thankfully, we had much to celebrate about Sarah's life. Sarah attained a position at an exclusive rehab facility. It was clear she was industrious, respected, and successful in her chosen field of addiction therapy. She was laying the groundwork for her own practice as a certified sex addiction therapist. She was a true survivor and reached out to help her afflicted brother.

Adam made an unexpected visit. He relapsed, was suicidal, and flew to us on a buddy pass on the way to Sarah's rehab facility, thanks to a scholarship she had generously arranged. He was going where the children of music stars and CEOs went to detox.

Watching your son with delirium tremens withdrawals in your guestroom is not easy. I provided him with a cool washcloth and a bucket should he get ill. We locked our bedroom door that night. Ryan told me he feared this cycle would never end. My heart ached for Adam, but it ached more for my husband. Ryan was ever the calm in the storm when dealing with crises. He did what he could for his errant son, praying for healing and strength and not passing judgment on Adam's past failures at sobriety. I saw this as a tremendous character strength and loved him more for it.

This episode did not give me much hope for Chad and Fern, who at this point *said* they were clean, though we didn't believe them. Many of our friends had the seemingly "perfect" children who had finished their educations, had careers, and were married. We often attended the weddings of our church choir friends' children. We doubted we would ever host our friends at any of our children's weddings, since ours were scattered far across the country, and for various reasons, disdained the idea of traditional marriage. We didn't feel needed much by our children.

Our dog filled our need to parent. He enjoyed a cozy lifestyle with frequent treats, plenty of toys, and a downy doggy bed. Since we had never owned a German shepherd before Rex, we studied up on the breed. We learned the average life span was twelve. For Rex's twelfth birthday, we treated him to a chicken entree and ice cream. We noticed he was having difficulty getting in and out of our car, and he slowed down on his walks to the park. Two weeks later, he suffered a stroke. He loved his rides in the car, so Ryan gave him one last, long ride before we put him down. Ryan wrote in his journal, "At 3:25 p.m. our beloved Rex departed this world." In retrospect, it was obvious our vet would tell us it was his time to go. We sobbed nonetheless.

"He was our love child together, the one who never asked for money," we reasoned.

He's over the rainbow bridge with Boots and Schatzie, where we will see him again.

Weeks afterward in 2010, Jessa and I went to a South Carolina beach for three days. Following this, she helped me to sprinkle Rex's ashes along the boardwalk where he loved to walk. Grief enveloped me, so while Ryan flew a long trip, I flew to visit Ford in his apartment on 88th and 2nd Avenue in the midst of bustling Manhattan. We strolled the MoMA together.

Soon afterward, Ryan and I drove to Johnstown to visit with Fern and Chad. Their apartment was clean and furnished, though meager. What better way to ease my grief at losing my Rex than to spend time with my three *human* children within the span of a few weeks?

***

My old friend Maggie from my second marriage invited us to her daughter's wedding reception. Ryan was flying, so I left several unreturned messages asking if my mother could attend in Ryan's place. The printed sheet of paper made no mention of the ceremony. Upon arrival, I was stunned to learn I wasn't invited to the wedding ceremony that day—a huge slight. Maggie and her husband were honored guests at Jessa's wedding. She must have bought into Wolf's badmouthing of me in her small town—a stinging betrayal by a once-best friend.

Shortly after Maggie met Ryan early in our relationship, she had told others that my motive for marrying him was money. Although I ignored her comments then, I could not overlook them now. She was no longer my friend. I told her so when she called me, months too late to offer her feeble explanation. I was honest with her about these two hurtful incidents. I have grown to value loyalty and honesty above all else in a friendship. Ryan has been my model. He is loyal to his university, to the US Navy, to his church, and most of all to the blessed people in his life.

CHAPTER TWENTY-TWO
Triple Play

Between Adam and Fern, our family was familiar with the cruel reality of addiction. I had written a play on this theme that was staged in downtown Pittsburgh. I rewrote it and applied for a county arts grant. The play was cast. A staged reading took place. The local drug awareness nonprofit with which I would split my profits endorsed it. Sadly, the grant was given to honor a play about a local artist, long dead, famous for creating cereal box characters. How naïve to think my effort to help save lives would win the prize. I would forever be a Yankee, not a native.

Greg's comic dinner theater roles beckoned to me. He wrote one with me in mind. *Southern Comfort* was his funniest yet, a spoof of Tennessee Williams' characters. I played Blanche du Bonkers—crazy, Southern, and over-sexed. Carol Burnett was my model. This role has been reprised several times. It is always satisfying to be paid for having so much fun being funny. An added bonus is befriending actors whose personalities and interactions add color and interest to the tapestry of one's life.

I wrote a comedic play, my attempt at a novel gift for Ryan. For years he came home telling of the best, worst, and oddest crew members with whom he worked. *Cockpit* was my one-act play based on these real characters and stories. The strait-laced captain role was modeled after Ryan. Tommy did not seem to want to produce it. I wore the producer hat by befriending the manager of the local theater, gathering a bunch of playwrights, and producing *7 at 8*—seven plays at eight o' clock. I also acted and directed in the production with my talented theater friends.

Then Greg pulled me into another of his creative ventures—his first movie, *Somebody Broke My Heart*. We filmed in city parks and on college campuses. My role was that of an eccentric lady in the park who was a reincarnation of Anne Boleyn. It was a sweet story and a novel experience for me. The movie premiered in an uptown theater. Dressed in a long black sequined gown, I sang the movie's plaintive title song into a microphone before many friends.

After we wrapped filming, a magazine came in the mail highlighted the best wine cellars in the country. When we looked up our state, we discovered a town in the mountains called Highlands. Why would this small town have so many renowned wine cellars? This resort town began as a retreat for the aristocracy of Atlanta. When the leaves were at their autumnal peak, we spent a weekend in an old inn there. We hiked trails that took us to five scenic waterfalls, browsed artsy shops, and ate sumptuous dinners with memorable wine, just as the magazine promised. And we noted that ours was the lone Chevy in parking lots full of luxury cars.

What really amazed us was the variety of well-trained dogs we saw throughout the town. We had been without our Rex for two months. When I spotted a fawn shepherd on the street, tears fell as the owner granted me permission to pet the dog. Meanwhile, Ryan engaged the owner in rapt conversation.

"A decision has been made as to what our next dog will be!" Ryan said over dinner.

"Which breed did you choose of the many that presented themselves?" I asked. I was ecstatic.

"At what point in the day did I take *any* interest at all in dogs? There is your big clue."

"But we already had our shepherd!" I protested.

"Ah, but he was not a Belgian Malinois shepherd!"

It did not take long to find Sky. He was a year-old, sable-coated purebred. He was slated for death in a shelter when a lady who runs a rescue saved him. She put him up on two websites, and it was instant love when we first set eyes on Sky. We flew to a city in Kentucky, rented a car, and began training him with an Arby's roast beef sandwich on the long trip home. He turned out to be the smartest dog we have ever known. Early in training class, he quickly grasped the commands of "sit," "stay," "down," "come," "heel," "turn," "fast," "slow," and "kiss."

It was as if he had mental telepathy with me. He was an innate protector, always wanting to be at our sides, ever alert and adoring. He was meant to be ours, and he was meant to be a therapy dog. He quickly sailed through classes and certification. He became part of a therapy dog team called PAWS. A dear lady named Maxine showed us the ropes at the local daycare facilities and nursing homes. When Ryan was not flying, he delighted in coming along.

Sky knew when he was going to provide therapy as soon as he saw his blue bandanna. He knew when folks needed love, were fearful of him, lonely, and even nearing death. My gorgeous dog channeled Christ's love in his actions. He strutted through hallways with Maxine's tiny Yorkie named AJ because they sensed they were best friends and teammates with a meaningful job to perform. And hilariously, the diminutive Yorkie was clearly the alpha dog.

***

Ryan switched back to international flying on the Airbus 330. As a first officer, he took a cut in pay but had a much nicer schedule. He had weekends off, alternating trips between Rome, Paris, and Frankfurt, rather than weekend red-eyes to the West Coast, landing at dawn. He flew me to Paris again, where we stayed on the top floor of a hotel overlooking the Eiffel Tower and the Arc de Triomphe. The entire crew ate a memorable meal together at La Petite Bistro in the quaint section of Mouffetard. We enjoyed the food and the laughter so much that the owner treated us. A free bottle of Sauvignon Blanc was placed before us. We sampled mushroom and brie crepes in Montmartre as we strolled by original art in the square. Maybe *we* were captured in a painting.

This trip was followed by a trip to Rome, where we climbed the Spanish Steps and walked to the Trevi Fountain, the Pantheon, and the Coliseum. Ryan proved Rome to be a walkable city, if one can endure eight miles of walking in one day! The stops for authentic pizza with sulfite-free vino, followed by coconut gelati, certainly helped to ease my pained feet. These memories of romantic times together in iconic cities cemented an otherwise stressful marriage. Soon we would be dealing with not only six children finding their way, but two octogenarians.

***

My parents visited in springtime of 2011 to look into area patio homes. We found one affordably priced in a quiet neighborhood. Mom, who made all financial decisions, was bothered by the empty lot next door. The retirement homes had less closet space than what she had at home, so they did not appeal to her. Her hoarding of clothes, shoes, and books worsened as she aged. She could not bear the thought of paring down her seventy jackets or eighty pairs of Dad's socks. No, really, I counted. There was no hope for changing her obsessive behaviors, as she refused to see them as such. I had dealt with her hoarding behavior my entire life. Closets, cabinets, and drawers were always haphazardly jammed with odds and ends, devoid of organization. It prompted me to be the opposite. I keep minimal contents in my closets, drawers, and pantry.

***

Adam called Ryan on his birthday to say he had been fired and was suicidal. What a birthday gift! He was at the hospital undergoing evaluation. After Ryan's first wife drove Adam there, she told him to stay away for six months. We felt no blame or judgment, as we certainly understood her frustration.

By summer, Adam was again in detox, but this time it was courtesy of the Salvation Army. We visited him and saw the meager compound where he was given three meals and a cot that he shared with lice. He could go through their program as long as he worked in the Florida sun six days a week and attended church on Sundays. One would hope this would be the place where he hit bottom. Jacob arranged to pick us up and take us to visit our twin grandsons while there. It was lovely to see the strong bond formed between the boys and their paternal uncle.

We made it a goal that summer to visit all of our children, spread far and wide and diverse in personality and lifestyle. We made a weekend visit to see Ford in his Midwest University town, surrounded by many good friends. We visited Fern when we accompanied her and Chad to the Flight 93 Memorial in Somerset, Pennsylvania. We visited Sarah when she attended a nearby conference in a job tailor-made for her. Most exciting was our visit to Nashville. Jessa and Jack told us the long-awaited news—that we would be grandparents again.

***

By not teaching acting, I had time to escape into my own theater projects. I won my first playwriting contest at the college where I had taught. I won my second playwriting contest with a one-act play, *The Comingling*, about a family gathering in a funeral parlor. A small theater company in North Carolina did a fantastic job producing this comedy that left audiences roaring.

Greg began filming a full-length film, *Above the Fire*, about the tenth anniversary of 9/11. My role was the grieving mother of a heroic fireman. I convinced Greg to cast Ford's girlfriend in a key role. She was my guest for a week. Her relationship with Ford would soon end, as she flirted with any admiring actor around her. The movie forever captured the park where we walked Sky at sunset. Sky had a brief role in the film with an ensemble cast. Greg produced an indie film on a tiny budget and paid me for my efforts. That is an artist's dream.

I began studying weekly with a fine arts master named Bolin. He teaches in a limited group setting at a bargain price. Bolin is a cross between Santa Claus and Sheriff Andy Taylor with the patience of Job. He has taught me more about drawing and painting than anyone. Bolin provides the discipline to paint regularly and the daring to try new techniques. The one man and two women who have been with me in his class have become invaluable friends and teachers themselves. My study with Bolin was rewarded when I began getting commissions for paintings.

Though the pressure was on to produce art for a paying customer, I had to pinch myself when I received my first check from a neighbor. I was getting paid to act *and* to create original art.

It sure beat any jobs I had been paid to do in the past.

CHAPTER TWENTY-THREE

Zinger

Ryan wanted me to experience sailing across the open ocean as he had in the Navy. We didn't want to try this on a small ship. We flew to Paris via our travel benefits and bought tickets at a discount from Air France to fly to Barcelona, our departure port. Many travelers do the same in autumn, then unbeknownst to us. We asked the help desk attendant about train service to Spain. She told us not to worry because if the captain allowed it, we could sit in the cockpit.

"Don't get too excited. You won't be able to sit there. You will see," Ryan told me.

We heard our names on the intercom, asking us to proceed to the end of the jetway.

A handsome French captain met us and said, "I vill be happy to hahv you up front."

No FAA regulation in France specifies who is allowed in the cockpit, so it *is* up to the captain. Tears of joy came to my eyes as we buckled up in cockpit jump seats. An attendant asked what kind of wine should arrive with our complementary salmon dinners…in the cockpit. *Pinch me!* I thought.

The crew pointed out landmarks of Paris for the most amazing aerial views in my life. We cleared the Pyrenees mountains to see the Barcelona airport in line with the coast. The next day we arrived at our aft-facing balcony room. The cruise first highlighted Italy's scenic western coast, followed by an ocean crossing to Miami, stopping at the Azores and Virgin Isles.

The huge ship had all the trappings of cruises—food trough buffets, gambling, too many bars, and efforts to convince you the shopping is all a bargain. But the days were unforgettable, even those with nothing but vast ocean for miles. Ryan relaxed while sharing stories I had never heard. He found joy in watching soft pastel sunsets, with his arms around me.

Not long after our return, Sky and I were making a pet therapy visit when Ford phoned me.

"I almost died last night," he said into the phone. "I got hit by a car while standing on the sidewalk and spent the night in Columbia Hospital. They say there are no broken bones or internal injuries," he told me.

I went home, packed, drove, and then broke down at the airline ticket counter. The agents put me in a first-row seat after I explained that a drunk driver had hit and run over my son when the car jumped a curb at high speed. Thankfully, an off-duty policeman apprehended the driver. If Ford had not been so tall and fit, having jumped high, it would have been his torso and not his calf that was run over. And why was he out late? He had just left a charity event with his friends. The tire track bruises were visible when he pulled up his pant leg to show me when I first entered his apartment.

I saw to it that he had groceries, I cleaned his kitchen, and we gave thanks at a local church. We believed he was spared for a reason, and we needed to pay this blessing forward. He told me that his new boss felt the same about this freak accident. Ford was making an impressive salary as an IT consultant and visited us after a month of healing, en route to Paris. He wanted to pursue his dream of owning his own tech start-up business, so he was taking a leave of absence. He told me how important it was for me to have faith in his dream, and my doubts and worries simply ceased.

***

As her Christmas gift to me that year, Fern handed me a journal inscribed with this: "In times of need I want you to write in this book. You always prayed for me when I needed you but I didn't know it. This book is to guide you in your times of need. Thank you for everything. If I didn't say it before, I am saying it now. Love, Fern."

Tears fell at reading her words, as her missteps took years away from our relationship. This was the first sincere thanks I had gotten from Fern in a long time. I had naïvely believed she and Chad were healed of addiction and would endure whatever hardships lay ahead of them.

***

The friends in my W-2 circle often ask if I miss working. My answer is that I find creative ways to work in our community. My second production of plays were performed at the local theater, *Deck the Halls with 7 One-Acts*. Greg and I starred in his play, *Presents Carefully Wrapped*, where we were siblings. We appreciated the irony since we had adopted each other as brother and sister. My play, *Santa's Dolly*, was about a mischievous elf planting an inflatable doll for Santa. Though the show was a success, my desire to produce plays ended after dealing with whiny actors who did not want to pull their share yet demanded equal pay. I dreaded creating budgets, schedules, and payouts.

I found organizing and acting in a live police training on mental illness more fulfilling. Actors role-played people in distress, some with mental illness needing specialized assistance, to educate public service trainees. For five years, I produced this live staged training, just as I continued to direct The Last Supper drama for my church. I still helped as needed with shows at Tommy's theater. These ventures fulfilled my need to serve my community. While Ryan was flying, I was doing what he told me to do when we first married…and loving it.

***

Ryan was taken off the line for two months, a mandatory precaution due to a change in heart medication. This provided for unexpected time to visit my folks and old friends. On this trip, we drove so that we could bring Sky along. Mom and Dad were able to see Sky at his best, doing pet therapy in their retirement community. A nursing home had named Sky volunteer of the month. My parents told us they wanted to move south to be near us, yet it seemed their main reason was lack of closet space. Coincidentally, we were becoming disillusioned with *our* neighborhood. We heard of a plan to put a new interstate exit by our development's entrance.

Homes had been robbed, and others were in foreclosure and disrepair. Our screened porch ceiling beams buckled from poor construction methods. Because of all this, at our request, our Realtors initiated a home search.

It didn't take long. They found a modern lake house with a finished basement apartment, a private third-floor master suite, and a common area overlooking a lush landscaped lawn. We took my parents to tour this home and hoped they would love it as much as we did.

"Who would want to live by that brown water?" Mom responded.

"A lake is not clear to the bottom like the Gulf of Mexico, Mom," I said in vain.

Ryan urged me to write up Mom's decision and send it in a letter, which I did. My attempt failed at moving them into a house wherein both couples could have their own access and privacy. The strain of this arrangement might have broken our marriage. My parents were never easy, and they were not mellowing in old age. They never really wanted to move south, except perhaps when they were experiencing a blizzard. From the onset of our marriage, we discussed that my responsibility would increase, along with our stress, as my parents declined. Dad always reminded me that his parents cared for his Irish grandmother and they cared for Nana Marie. It was truly a relief that our offer had been rejected, but at least we'd *made* an offer.

At the same time we were contemplating having my parents with us, Jessa was pregnant. I was more a nervous wreck than she was due to memories of the tragedy of my first birth. But, on the first day of spring, 2012, my world brightened when our grandson, Gray, was born. An early call from Jack awakened me, I got on a plane, and four hours later, all nine pounds, seven ounces of Gray arrived. Healthy and blond, with sky-blue eyes, he turned my heart to pure goo at first sight. Jessa commenced motherhood with total organization and strict schedules. She took three months of maternity leave. How thrilling it was to have him all to myself the first week that Jessa returned to work. I couldn't wait to create my first portrait of Gray, asleep in a basket.

On the same trip, we visited with Sarah, who was excelling at her job outside of Nashville, supervising more than sixty employees who serve wealthy clients with addictions. She gave us a tour of the facility, where we met her loyal and capable staff. This young woman had turned around her own struggles to help others do the same. Empathic and compassionate, Sarah is a healer of many aching souls and she makes us very proud parents.

***

During Gray's first summer, Fern and Chad took a ride to the Maryland lake house of Jack's parents to meet her new nephew. Jessa summed up the reunion: "Fern looked dangerously thin and sounded scattered." Jessa treated teens who were addicted to drugs and knew the look. And sadly, she was seeing a condition similar to that of her father who left us sixteen years prior.

***

We flew to Florida to visit with Adam and Jacob. They were not on speaking terms, probably due to the fact that Jacob was now the primary male role model for Adam's sons. Their sharing of a condo had left Jacob in the lurch financially. The relationship between the brothers was sadly strained beyond repair. Ryan could do nothing to alter this.

Shortly after our visit, Adam called us on our fifteenth anniversary but not in congratulations. He had relapsed and was returning to the Salvation Army. The last time he relapsed, six men from our church met for an hour-long prayer vigil, praying for his deliverance from addictions and suicidal thoughts. I believed the men had worked a miracle through prayer. Although this call dashed my timeline for Adam, I held tight to my faith in God's timeline. A couple doesn't want to remember the timeline of relapses, rehabs, and divorces of their children. But when it coincides with a celebratory day in your life, it is harder to forget. This was cruel.

Adam had abused his asthmatic, frail body with toxins too numerous to mention. I remember reading a fortune cookie slip that said, "Old Chinese Proverb: May your children outlive you." It is a fortune every parent wants to actualize, but many do not. Then the pain haunts them every day thereafter. *Would Ryan outlive Adam?* I wondered. *Would I outlive Fern?*

CHAPTER TWENTY-FOUR

Another Timeout

Our friends and Realtors, Deb and Jill, negotiated a four-story townhouse closer to the lake. The temperature on the day we first saw the home was 105 degrees, so it appealed mightily to rid ourselves of the responsibility of outside maintenance. We fixed up our first southern home and sold it quickly at a loss, yet we purchased our new home well under its value. We were ready to move two interstate exits north, closer to the airport and closer to the Queen City. We moved, but not far—from the south to the southeast shore of the same lake.

We loved our new, easier home. The light streamed into the living room through three sets of French doors. A stargazing, sunset-viewing deck awaited us off the top guest suite. In case Fern ever truly hit bottom and needed to start over, that area would be hers for the asking. But for now, our only dependent was our loyal shepherd Sky, who happily joined us in exploring the walking trails by the lake and through the woods of the new neighborhood.

Ford was our first guest. He attended my last acting performance at Tommy's theater. My character was a mother of two daughters, one a drug abuser and one who was a resentful, yet obedient over-achiever. Jessa had indeed become resentful of Fern's lifestyle and the energy it zapped from us. With what I went through with my own daughters, this role was a little too close to home. Tommy refused again to produce my play *The Comingling*, which had been successfully produced elsewhere. Tommy did not seem to miss my absence from his theater, so I moved on to work exclusively with Greg.

Above the Fire premiered at the choice movie theater of downtown Charlotte. Not only did Greg and I sell this film to the proprietors, but we also delivered on our promise to fill the theater. The movie's poster at the city's famous crossroads of Trade and Tryon during the 2012 Democratic National Committee's convention featured my tearful face. My friends attended in support. Seeing my character on-screen felt eerie as I saw myself mourning my on-screen son's death in dysfunctional ways. Yet Greg's forte is in character development. What an honor to give birth to his words even if my character's on-screen behavior *was* quite nasty. Spoiler alert: I attempt to strangle my husband to death.

***

Ryan and I stood at an altar in Nashville to see Gray baptized at nine months of age. Afterward, while another relative held him, he saw me, cried out, and lunged toward me. My heart was bursting with grandma love. He's an answer to our prayers for a healthy, gorgeous, and intelligent grandchild. Besides kisses and snuggles, he loved singing and dancing with Gammylee, as he dubbed me.

The toddler affection he offered was similar to what I felt from Fern so long ago. As my mother used to say, Fern was the "love bug" of my three. She finally ended her relationship with Chad. A friend offered to train her toward managing his fast-food restaurant near our home. Instead, she chose to live with her dour supervisor of a discount clothing store. I prayed she would someday leave the depressed drug-infested city where she lived.

***

My folks were curious to see our new home, so we met them at the Pittsburgh airport and escorted them south using our buddy passes. Since Mom always overpacked, this was not easy.

"We love your new home. When can Mom and I move in?" Dad asked me.

"We found the house for that arrangement. You declined. This one just will not do," I told him.

They were in the best place to live out their days, especially as their health declined. Mom told me she needed help organizing her clothes, so I returned with them to assist her.

I spent hours trying to put a small dent in Mom's hoarding. An administrator said we needed to clear a path from the bedroom to the bathroom, per the institutional safety requirements. Mom would never pay a professional to help her. Sleep eluded me on her sofa after I lugged many bags down to the trash room. Mom informed me that I was cruel and she told me not to come back, even though I patiently gave her a choice with every item when I held it up before her eyes. "Do you wear it? Need it? Love it?" I asked these three questions *all day long*.

As a World War II vet, Dad wanted to attend his 507th Parachute Infantry Regiment reunion in Georgia. Ryan and I drove them to the reunion in the comfort of our new car with a "talking computer," over which they marveled. We made the trip in an effort to keep Dad from driving his own car, a scary proposition over such a long distance. Their road trip days were numbered, even as passengers, so Ryan viewed it as his military mission, while I viewed it more as my daughterly duty. After dropping them off at the reunion, we spent two nights at a secluded lodge and then attended the final reunion breakfast with Dad and thirteen other World War II vets. When nearing our home, Dad casually offered this conversation starter.

"We think your cousin Gayle in Florida genuinely wants us to live with her."

"Her mom stole your inheritance, signing yours over to her," I said, reminding them.

Then Mom projected her feelings of failure onto me when she said I called her a failure.

"Mom, your *perception* is that I made you feel that way because there was no one else to help you to declutter other than me."

"Well, I *may* have too many clothes, but my real problem is not enough closet space."

At this point, I felt like we were residing on two different planets, in different galaxies.

The next day at a restaurant, first Dad yelled at me when I suggested he order a $21 entrée, then he took his teeth out at the table, wiping them with a napkin. He got angry when I called him rude. Mom said he just figured no one would see. I told her not to make excuses. Ryan said the whole experience was surreal since Dad's loud and rude filter was seldom on.

That memorable weekend made me vow to be kinder as old age descends. I do not want to emotionally exhaust my children. At least we came home to our sweet dog, who helped us through this difficult phase of life. But then, shortly after our return, we got the terrible news that Sky had histiocytic sarcoma of the blood. What the vet first thought was a routine kennel cough was due to massive tumors in his lungs. Sky was just four years old.

Ford got a flight Christmas Eve and stayed with us for three precious days of support. Sky held on through Christmas, but the tumors grew quickly, affecting his breathing. On Christmas morning Sky was bleeding all over our white carpeting. Sadness enveloped me as I cleaned it up. Later that day, Ryan's sister took one last photo of us with Sky. The next day we found ourselves in the same room where we experienced Rex's last moments years before. We held Sky's head and stroked him as he died peacefully. A snippet of his fur remains nestled in his blue bandanna in my nightstand, feet from where we sleep. We will never have a dog as intelligent as Sky, and we suffered through his unexpectedly early loss. My grandparents and Aunt Peg, who were *all* dog lovers, are making good use of this certified therapy dog in Heaven.

***

Ryan and I visited Jessa and Jack's new home on the edge of a golf course. During this visit, Jessa told me she connected with her biological father through Facebook.

They arranged a meeting at a Waffle House in Kentucky. After a quarter century apart, they reunited, per his request. Jack said she was cold and distant and did not share her address. She simply met a prematurely aged man at a restaurant who is her biological father and no more. Jessa saw how my marriage to Jon had been destined to fail and how much more blessed our lives were with Ryan as a husband, father, grandfather, and role model. This meeting, though surprising, sounded as pitiful as Jon's email exchange with Ford years earlier.

***

Ford had no desire for such a meeting with his biological father. He was too busy fueling his dreams of entrepreneurialism, motivated by his unhappy restlessness acting as an IT consultant. Although based in New York City, he was sent away on assignments for months at a time. He took a project in Amsterdam where he had a liberal expense account and plenty of free time to work on his dream of starting his own company. His employer urged him to visit European cities on weekends. He had the chance to see many exotic places, but this job fell far short of his entrepreneurial passion.

This prompted me to visit Ford in Amsterdam. He was living in a historic, luxurious canal house. We visited the Anne Frank House, art museums, the red-light district, historic castles, and the canal system via a narrated barge ride. It was springtime and a rainbow spectrum of tulip colors were in bloom everywhere we walked. The odor of marijuana overwhelmed us as we passed cafes where it is eaten instead of smoked. The Dutch are too intelligent to damage their lung tissue. In fact, an elderly native told us they leave the buying of sex and drugs to the foreigners. They know better. But they appreciate these revenues coming into their country.

After that glamorous assignment, Ford resigned from his six-figure job and moved into a Brooklyn brownstone to fully develop his business proposals. I had no worries about his future. He was forward-thinking in his inventive business proposals and knew how to connect to exactly the right investors.

Fern called to say she would be moving due to her new job at a restaurant. So, that summer, we drove to Johnstown. We surprised Fern at the restaurant where she was one of three sushi chefs. She *was* surprised but not quite in the way we had hoped. When I cried and wanted a hug, she got angry and said I was going to get her in trouble. She gave us her update robotically while we stood in front of the sushi bar:

"I'm in debt on college loans, so I live upstairs over the restaurant. The cook is my roommate and he's a slob. There is nothing in my living room, not even a sofa, and I need a car. I've gained twenty pounds eating free here, so I've saved over three grand. And that's my life."

I was relieved to hear only her last detail, as she was way too thin and hadn't been a saver. After pausing for a deep breath, I asked if she could come home for Christmas.

"My Christmas break is three days. That's it. The boss pays me double what I last made, under the table, weekly."

At this point, this boss approached me and asked why I was crying. I told him it was simply joy at seeing my daughter after such a long time. While Fern was working, he told me she was doing better because he was strict and keeping her busy, away from "scum" she was with. He said he invited her to his church and he was a man of God with a young daughter. He assured me he would tell her to meet with us for breakfast. He may have told her, but she didn't meet us.

After she received her birthday card with a modest check, Fern "friended" us on Facebook. That was our only connection to her. Later, I discovered Fern's post to "Save the Date." Could she already be marrying the new boyfriend she mentioned on Facebook? My text told her that we were praying for good news. Then a text clarified her meaning.

"The good news is," she wrote, "on that date my new boyfriend is getting out of jail, something you would not understand or think is good news."

We were blindsided by this tidbit of information.

I replied, "Whenever someone gets out of jail, it is good news. If you are happy, so am I."

Fern's life now revolved around Brian. She used up her ample savings to buy him supplemental meals and phone calls while he was in jail. She would not be visiting us because, in her words, "Brian will be in outpatient drug rehab, and I will not visit you without him."

Similarly depressing, we finally heard from Jacob, when he suddenly visited us in our new home. He convinced Ryan to sell him our old car for the amount of an insurance check he received for his recently totaled car. Using our travel pass to arrive, Jacob retrieved the car and spent one obligatory night with us before leaving early the next morning. He was clearly uncomfortable in our home and did not communicate much about his life, unless we asked pointed questions of him. It was the last time he would ever visit us. It was clear that he made the journey this time only because he desperately needed a car.

CHAPTER TWENTY-FIVE
Pickle

I attended my fortieth high school reunion with Ryan and Sharon. My high school beau, Bobby, traveled all the way from Florida. There is always a fascination to see your first crush at reunions. Divorced with three sons, he is now an entomologist for US Customs. Ryan was considerate, giving us ten minutes to catch up while he went to listen to the band play '70s favorites. Bobby shared his misfortunes in life with me. He was also divorced; one of his sons was an addict and another was serving time. We both described how bizarre it was seeing how our home town had morphed into a bustling Yuppieville, barely recognizable from our memories.

***

Fern called after Christmas to say she had lost her job and her apartment because Brian had stayed overnight. According to Fern, her boss was a lecherous ogre. It was his restaurant and his apartment, and therefore his rules. I told her he had claimed he was a man of God who took her to his church. She said that this never happened. Rather, he had offered to pimp Fern out as a prostitute to his rich friends, where she could make much more money on the side. She told him in no uncertain terms that he was a pig. I followed up her call with this letter, in which I subdued my emotions and worries for her:

Daily prayers are said that you and Brian get jobs and that he sails through rehab and stays clean. Your texts came to me while I was in Germany with Ryan on his last trip as a first officer. He will now fly domestic as a captain for the remainder of his career as a pilot.

We prefer not to help with cell minutes, but we will help with medicine, doctor visits, food, basic needs. It was unfair of your boss to leave you jobless and homeless over Brian. Please stay away from this hateful man who has nothing but evil to offer you. We are grateful for Brian's mom's kindness of taking you into her home. We'd do the same if you lived near us.

Weeks passed with nothing from Fern. Then she called, once again asking for help.

"It's your job to buy my basic needs cause Brian's mom has no choice but to take me in. Brian told his mom if I don't move in, she'll never see him again."

This felt like a scenario in a Dear Abby letter. We imagined what advice would be given.

We did not see it as our job to support her. She gave her word to reconnect to family but offered only a brief letter to her grandmother. Fern expected us to send her money, yet she rarely acknowledged us. We told Fern we would buy her a used car only if she lived with us.

"Why should I communicate with you if you do not give me money?" she snapped.

What a jolt to my heart! Was I only a money source? Surely, she was still using drugs. On Facebook, she sported a huge tattoo of black roses covering her bony shoulder. My heart ached, seeing this "body art" appearing on Fern's unblemished, tawny skin.

When life handed me this pickle, something sweet came with it. Jessa told us to expect another grandson by sending a photo of Gray bawling in a chair and holding a sign saying he would be getting a baby brother. Her due date was April 30. I predicted that the event would occur on April 22, Ford's birthday. My grandson, Cole, made his arrival into this world at ten pounds, seven ounces on this very day. Jessa had the baby just minutes after getting to the hospital.

***

We flew to Nashville post haste to meet Cole and chuckle at Gray, who did not know what to make of the red, noisy bundle screaming in a blanket. I tried to soothe Gray by giving him a gift. Gray opened his first acrylic painting from his Gammylee. The subject was Gray at the wheel of his favorite little blue truck. For a two-year old, he spent much time examining the colors and details of the painting. This was a precursor of the artistic talent he'd go on to exhibit.

Cole was a colicky baby who awakened every two hours to nurse. It predictably stressed Jessa to be dealing with a demanding baby and a jealous two-year-old. When I thought back to my early years of motherhood, I found solace that my daughter had it better, with a husband who loves her in a comfortable, elegant home. God blessed us with another healthy, handsome grandson, whose round blue eyes and golden curls much more resembled Jessa as a baby.

***

We celebrated Ryan's sixtieth birthday with thirty-five friends in our neighborhood community room. Food, wine, and laughter were present with many speaking highly of my humble husband. I wanted Ryan to know that he is the answer to my prayers, so I shared these heartfelt words:

I have a frame where I keep our photo. It reads, "Once in a while, right in the middle of an ordinary life, love gives us a fairy tale. Seventeen years ago tonight, I took you out to dinner while wearing my red dress. You gave the toast, 'May all your shooting star wishes come true.' That is when the tears came into your eyes. That is when I fell in love with you. We came true. Ryan, my Captain America, my best friend, happy sixtieth birthday."

***

Another big birthday was nearing, Dad's ninetieth. I feared he may not reach it due to his congestive heart failure worsening. Edema and labored breathing led him to test at the VA hospital for a new surgical procedure, which is standard procedure today. His aortic valve would be replaced with one made of pig and cow tissue. I visited him during this preparatory testing, offering to help Mom with the huge piles of clothes in her bedroom, but she declined my offer.

I drove her each day to the hospital and offered to help with ironing. Mom wanted everything ironed before finding a place for it, but this was merely a diversionary tactic. *Then* I burned a hole in a pair of polyester pants, which never even required ironing. I said a quick prayer: "It's too late to wish for a normal mother, but Lord could you help me to be one? And please don't let me ever put insignificant things before relationships."

"They are polyester! I feel horrible, but at least they weren't expensive!" I blurted.

That, apparently was a shot to her ego, and she unleashed a veritable tempest toward me. We went to lunch, where she wanted to discuss how deeply I had upset her. She had a long list, following a cathartic discussion, all of which I recounted in my journal that evening.

"You hurt me by saying the pants weren't expensive," she began. "Since you married Ryan, you have changed! You are money-conscious. Nothing we have is good enough. You have no compassion for older people. You make me feel like a failure. [her mantra] When you come, you never stay long, and Ryan just sits there like a lump!"

Or, I thought, *a wise Buddha!*

"Do you ever say things that hurt me?" I added, unleashing my elephant in the room.

"What have I *ever* said to hurt you?" she asked, dumbfounding me, as my head bobbed.

"Well, it started at age five with, 'You will never be as pretty as Sharon,'" I answered.

"Sharon *was* a pretty girl. And my mother *never* told me I was pretty."

Ouch, it still hurt.

"You continued a wrong. I told my daughters constantly that they were beautiful," I said.

"Dad never believed Jon was an alcoholic," she said after a period of silence.

This was the biggest slam of all, implying that I was the sole cause of our divorce.

"We always supported you and never disowned you," she added.

At this point I froze. Had she been living in an alternative universe with another daughter? For two years following college, we had literally not spoken due to my interracial relationship. Their support through failed marriages was minimal at best with no financial help and plenty of criticism. I took another deep breath and formulated how to answer succinctly with the truth.

"Yes, you did, over Vernon," I said. She was drawing a blank. I added, "He was black."

"Well, we were not proud of you then. How would you have felt?" she defended.

"I have no problem with dating outside of one's race. At least he wasn't a prisoner."

"So we were wrong?" she asked tight-lipped, trying to defend her indefensible beliefs.

"Yes, bigotry is wrong." I stated the obvious. I was the teaching adult in the room.

"But the children suffer terribly in a mixed marriage!" she said, unable to let it go.

"Mom, one of them is our president, who you voted for! He is doing quite well," I said.

"That boyfriend was why your grandma never gave you her silver and coral bracelet!"

"You continued the wrongs of a proudly bigoted Irishwoman who you could not stand?"

"Well, we have unresolved issues. We were good parents. *You* made mistakes," she said.

"I made plenty. I fully admit that. Just give me the lunch tab." I could not win, so I paid.

Then and there this memoir commenced as a therapeutic reality check of my life.

***

Weeks later, Dad's operation was a success, and he enjoyed a swift recovery. My visit lasted five days. Upon my return home, Mom phoned, asking me to fly back just to lift her mattress. She said she had been bitten by a spider, but the nurse assured me this simply was not the case. In conversation with the totally confounded nurse, all I could tell her was, "Welcome to my world."

CHAPTER TWENTY-SIX
Fielder's Choice

On a visit to see my adorable, clever grandsons, I realized how much I had missed of my own little boy's childhood. From when Ford was Gray's age on, I was filled with worry over paying bills, my career, and raising three children alone. Wolf had never stepped up to the role of father. Despite this absence, Ford was quite a creative and motivated young man. He launched his tech start-up, which took off due in part to a new partner moving the company to San Francisco and securing more investors. Ford explained he was living in tech start-up Mecca—though he was awfully far away from his mother!

On Ryan's next layover there, we visited with him. Ford's "office" was steps away from his bedroom where his work attire was a T-shirt and flip-flops. After our arrival, he walked us to a trendy oyster bar and excitedly told us of the birth and growth of a company he and his friends had created. He was thriving in a city where his entrepreneurial dream might just come true someday.

***

Our vacation destination dream was about to come true. Seeing animals in their natural environment is what *this* vacation was all about. The Galapagos Islands look like Jurassic Park…on the moon's surface. Our first day there, we saw giant turtles roaming amidst farmers' fields. The rules are no touching, feeding, or getting too near these gentle, protected creatures.

The magic of the Galapagos Islands is that though the animals are not tame, they are completely indifferent to humans. They look at visitors as if to ask, "Why are you in my neighborhood?"

We explored four main islands over four days on a ship with twenty-nine passengers and three naturalists. My hope was to swim with sea lions. We did just that on our first dip into the sea. The juvenile was a frisky pup that became jealous when we diverted our gaze to a turtle. The sea lion swam up to within inches of our bodies and blew bubbles in our awed, masked faces.

As we snorkeled, we saw a massive Galapagos shark below us as well as a huge manta ray, a spotted eagle ray, giant sea stars, and rainbow parrotfish. Marine iguanas dove by us while they fed on algae. In shallow water, a petite Galapagos penguin swam circles around me in my furnished wet suit. The guide told us never to worry about being eaten…we are not tasty enough.

We took hikes up steep cliffs over lava rock and climbed the summit of Pinnacle Rock. From that vantage point, we saw what appeared to be a hawk killing a baby sea lion. Then the naturalist walked us over to within feet of the animals. We saw the hawk was eating the placenta. We felt as if we were watching a National Geographic television special, only we were there live, seeing it firsthand. We soaked in every memory of this wild paradise, which wowed us.

The undersea adventure is only half of the expedition. The other is the birds. We climbed a cliff and walked across a mesa to see the most unusual display. We had to step around hundreds of birds as they squawked at us, not in annoyance, but in their greeting of curiosity.

Nazca, blue and red-footed boobies, frigate birds, pelicans, petrels, owls, gulls, tropical birds, herons, and of course, Darwin's finches were just a few of the birds we enjoyed. To explore these islands, one must be fit to snorkel and hike for hours. Ryan, who does not like to snorkel, was all the braver on the last day of dangerous, choppy, cloudy surf, swimming among hammerhead sharks he could not see! We felt blessed to go on this expedition, one we had studied up on beforehand with fascination. We returned with a greater appreciation for the diversity of nature.

When we returned, I dialed Fern's phone number. It was no longer a working number. She had gotten what she wanted, once again—a total disconnection from her family, who had no way to contact her. The slogans of our old support group came to mind: Let go and Let God. We had to trust that "In God's Time," she would have an epiphany, "Find a New Playground," and return, hopefully free of addiction, to her family.

***

When we visited on Dad's ninetieth birthday, both my parents were getting around primarily by scooter, but Mom still had not made a doctor's appointment for her swollen knee, so I made one. At the doctor's office, we learned she was not a surgery candidate at her age and condition. She would live the rest of her days in pain with every step. Lesson learned? Knee replacements wear out over time just like our God-given knees do.

We threw dad a well-attended party in their community's atrium with refreshments and balloons, gave him a pocket watch, and took many photos of him with his friends and staff.

Ryan heard Mom say, "That's my daughter. She's been married three times."

Oh please, Mom! Was this running introductory put-down a conversation starter, a way to continually dig at me, or did she want to find a friend who had a child who had done the same? I will never know. I was tempted to say, "Actually, I have been married six times. There were three you've never known of."

Ford told me later that Dad had told *him* that I was an amazing woman. At least *Dad* was grateful for my efforts.

***

During our first Christmas celebration with no children visiting, Ryan and I made the most of romance, spending extra time in our marital bed. We sang at our Christmas Eve service and celebrated with two neighboring couples afterward. We felt disheartened not to hear from Jacob, Sarah, or Fern. Sarah's excuse was that she had lost her phone on Christmas Day. We don't believe we've ever neglected to call our parents on Christmas, as we certainly did that day also.

Ryan received this private chat message just after Christmas: "Merry Christmas. I don't ever get on Facebook 'cause I don't have a phone or money to get one. Doing the best I can. Love you and Mom. Tell her I'm fine. Fern."

This took me back to the years after Jon abandoned us, when he would send his children just a Christmas card and write, "I love you." An audible snicker escaped my lips every time. The gall of him merely scrawling that to his own children, whom he had not visited in decades! Divorce fractures families, plain and simple. It takes patience and work to glue the pieces back together. Step-parenting has unique challenges. I imagine being a step-child feels just as awkward and artificial, especially through the beginning years of a new second or third union. But once the adult children see that the marriage will endure and makes their parent happy, their rebellion at the union should decrease, and their comfort level should increase. One can always hope for this realization.

After the holiday air traffic died down, we were long overdue to visit with Gray and Cole. Gray didn't take long to snuggle into my arms, producing an endorphin rush in his grandma.

"Gammylee, are you gonna sing the 'Gray Song?'" he cooed, melting me.

I had made up a song to sing to him as a newborn to the tune of "Love is Blue." I sang it to him at each visit, but this was the first time I knew *he* remembered, even anticipated, our song.

The second melting of my heart was when he realized I was leaving the next day. His big, blue eyes looked straight at me. "I'm gonna miss you so bad!" he cried out, and instant tears flooded my eyes.

Cole, meanwhile, was laughing, imitating, and making new sounds as a bright, adorable two-year-old.

***

Ryan took me on an overnight work trip to Long Beach, California. The actual flight was to LA, but bedbugs in the usual crew hotel forced the crew to stay aboard the *Queen Mary*, a British luxury liner built in 1936. This ship is huge, having bunked more than sixteen thousand troops during World War II. We enjoyed the ship as well as the harbor and downtown area. The rooms were crafted in fine hardwoods. After dining in the on-board restaurant, we slept in this ship museum. It was worth the jet lag even though I had only one night in my own bed before we flew again.

***

We visited our twin grandsons in Florida for an annual 5K race for Cerebral Palsy named for them. It was awkward to see their mother, who had every reason to disallow Adam's visitation.

A TV station covered the event and interviewed the boys, then age seven. Their mom assisted them in crossing the finish line. We jogged half the race and felt sore for days following.

I referred to Ryan as Jacob's dad as I took a photo. To explain that Ryan is Adam's dad and thus their grandpa would have been hurtful to them, reminding them of their dad's absence on this day. *We* felt hurt also as we never heard from Adam, though he knew of our travel plans.

We had a pleasant day with Jacob as he drove us in our old car to a quaint seafood cafe and then to stroll through a crowded art fair. He confirmed that Adam had relapsed. The mystical moment on this day was seeing Adam pull up to an intersection on his bike as we were passing. It was God's way of telling us he is alive and well. Jacob certainly did not want to stop, as he only heard from his brother when Adam called asking for cigarette money.

Jacob seemed content with his journalism career, splitting a house with his roommate, and with his friendships centering around his frequent music gigs. I gently asked him to call his father more, though my asking had the reverse effect. That day in 2015 was the last time we saw or heard from Jacob. But we were not alone. He then "divorced" his mother, siblings, and even his adoring nephews. How truly sad.

CHAPTER TWENTY-SEVEN
A Perfect Game

Ryan and I attended a musical matinee in Charlotte where a kind lady sat by us. She said she headed a foundation for folks who lose contact with their adult children. Was she an angel guiding me?

"Imagine not hearing from your child for a year!" she said to me during the intermission.

In fact, we lived that scenario. The following day, I searched for the phone number of the home of Brian's mother. Though I had searched for it in the past, it magically appeared when I opened the kitchen junk drawer. Doesn't everyone have such a drawer?

Fern answered this number on the first ring. I had questions to ask her and, for the first time, she did not avoid answering them. She still lived with Brian's mom and was not employed. She still needed thyroid medication, an antidepressant, and weekly counseling at a clinic. She still had no desire to leave Johnstown.

"I haven't been in touch 'cause there is no good news, Mom."

"It leaves a hole in my heart to not hear from you. A mother worries," I told her, again.

"You have to get over that, Mom. You can call me next week. I love you," she said.

What a relief to have reestablished weekly communication, although I was anxious and hesitant about what to say. So much damage had been done by drugs, distance, misperceptions, and altered memories. I mailed her a Walmart gift card and a print of a pencil portrait I had drawn. She seemed more positive and grateful with each call. Taking baby steps was working.

Fern invited us to visit her and to meet Brian and his father. She was delighted to give us the news of her new job at a jewelry store. We immediately planned a visit on her next day off.

The weather was unusually sunny on our drive from the airport. Within minutes of our arrival, she was at our hotel door, my lovely, happy, thirty-year-old Fern. The beauty lost a decade ago was before me. She warned me not to cry, and that did not happen until I got a hug from Brian and thanked him for taking care of her. Sitting in our hotel room, Brian won us over with his honesty in disclosing his past troubles and family dynamics. We took Fern and Brian out for dinner at the nicest eatery we could find, at the top of their small, hilly city.

They both were excited at the thought of visiting our home and vacationing with our family. Brian fervently related his faith and daily prayer to us. Fern was healthy and cared for.

For years my prayer for Fern was to come back to me. But what if she came back disabled, or worse, from an overdose? With every discussion came more revelations. She was undergoing counseling to understand why she had made such poor decisions and had reacted in ways hurtful to family members. The old, affectionate Fern had returned. She wanted to reconnect, to forgive and be forgiven, and to share her life with us. The loss of a decade of her life was painful, but she was working to rebuild our trust by knitting back the stitches of our relationship, one at a time. There was peace within me at last concerning the welfare and future of Fern.

***

We visited my parents on my mother's birthday. Dad met us at the door demanding we take Mom home with us. They had difficulty getting up from their chairs and into our car. Despite having a new closet built in their living room, we did not see much progress with the de-hoarding. Mom granted permission to throw out one box of books, years-old herbs and spices, and long-expired canned goods, although she said, "Those dates they stamp on there don't mean a thing!"

***

I was determined that at my sixtieth birthday celebration, I would be easy on my children. It began with a call from Ford as I stepped into the shower.

"There is a deliveryman at your door trying to give you a present."

"Just how do you know this, Ford? I'm in my bathrobe and do not want to go down now!"

"An app tells me, Mom. He's been on the phone with me. He is really nice. Go down."

When I got downstairs, Ford was there, surprising me. He flew in early from Salt Lake City and called Uber. I enjoyed his company for five days. He told me he was in negotiations to sell his company to a billion-dollar tech firm, providing he accepted a full-time salaried position overseeing a new division involving his product. His dream *was* about to come true, and I knew what this meant to Ford. My son had brilliant ideas and a huge need to be creative and make a difference in the tech world. His father had deserted him, so he had made his own path, in his own way. He was a good man, grounded and loving. My prayers for him were about to be answered. But not a word could be uttered about it to anyone, until the lawyers finalized the sale.

When Ryan returned from his work trip, he brought my college brother Gary with him from the airport. Gary was losing his eyesight to macular degeneration, yet he faced it with humor and gratitude as an example to all who love him. Jessa and Cole flew in for the weekend. Unfortunately, Fern didn't have the luxury of a job that afforded her days off to travel.

All was going well in preparing for my birthday dinner party with dear friends when my kitchen sink backed up. On our first level, the main sewage pipe was blocked and overflowed from the bathtub into the guest suite with raw sewage everywhere. Neighbors allowed our guests to take showers while professionals cleaned the biohazard. Shit happened—literally.

We arrived at a local restaurant, semi-relaxed with cake and flowers. There were three large tables of family and friends. Ryan was the perfect host, praying out loud for "my wife, who has blessed all of our lives." Cole was perfectly behaved. I showed off his big blue eyes to all.

A call came from the one I loved who could not be present. Fern wished me well, then spoke with Ford, who gently asked her all the questions we all had pondered, in the right way.

***

My son and I are both extroverts, open with our thoughts and emotions. We are aware this can be our strength, as well as our weakness. Ford is blessed to have gotten his father's good looks, and his beautiful red hair. I thank God every day he got my creative brain, with no dangerous addictions, unless you count rock climbing. He assures me he uses safety equipment!

***

The next year of my life would be the last year wherein I could accompany my working pilot husband without being needed by my parents. Besides visiting a half dozen American cities I had never seen before, I most relished flying to Salt Lake City to see Ford, Nashville, to see Jessa, and Pittsburgh to see my folks and Fern. Ryan's airline provided for my air and hotel expenses, a much-appreciated spousal benefit with a family as geographically spread out as ours. We next would use his benefits to fly across the globe.

Our next big vacation was a cruise on the Baltic Sea. First, we flew into Oslo, where we boarded a ship that took us to Helsinki, Gdansk, St. Petersburg, Latvia, and Lithuania, ending in Stockholm. We experienced unexpected drama in Wismar, Germany. We took a biking side trip on rural island pathways. Ryan fiddled with his camera and in the process fell hard onto gravel. He bruised ribs and lost a lot of skin on his forearm. We had our own unplanned field trip to a small-town German hospital, miraculously getting aboard the ship before it set sail. At least I spoke their language, albeit like a child. Surprisingly, neither the ambulance driver nor the doctor spoke English as well as I did German. We communicated slowly and patiently, out of necessity. Thankfully there were no lasting effects from the fall and we were able to enjoy the time away.

***

When I return from traveling, I am often inspired to paint. Paintings can be like cooking creations. Sometimes they may turn out unique with an amazing blend of flavors, and other times, you vow never to make that combination of blah again. I painted a rather large Siberian tiger lolling in the grass and it is my favorite to this day. It was displayed at a local gallery, one named for that welcoming gentleman Harry that we met so long ago when visiting our church. Following this honor, Ryan encouraged me to transform a room in our home into a gallery and hold my own opening. On that occasion, a friend bought my painting of an old copper pot. It was gratifying to see talented artist friends attend to encourage the continuance of my artwork.

This event prompted me to give my old lover Will a call to tell him of my current years as a fledgling artist, inspired by his success. He was surprised to hear this voice from long ago. I extended an invitation to him to visit us if ever passing through. He told me of his extremely jealous wife, who would not take to that idea. Incredibly, five years older than me, he was raising four young children with a much younger woman from a faraway land. He gave me his blessing to tell our story, and I wished him well. Our love seemed from a long-ago dream and so inconsequential. Yet, looking back, we both felt our affair was a necessary step in our journey toward appreciating our current mates all the more. Ryan would never be the life of the party, the best dancer in the room, or a renowned sculptor, as Will was.

But Ryan was steady as a rock in his loyalty and commitment to me, to our children, to our Lord. My priorities had certainly changed.

CHAPTER TWENTY-EIGHT
Rocking Chair Position

My seventh decade began in April with a storm involving my parents that lasted more than two years. Just at the time we felt that our adult children's lives just might take on a Zen-like peace, the demands of my parents would be yet another test on my patience as a daughter and on my marriage. The professionals at their retirement community determined they should move from independent living to assisted living. They both needed to have medications dispensed and ongoing physical therapy sessions as their falls had increased. In addition, they needed to dispose of electrical items and maintain clear pathways in their apartment. This was standard procedure.

Of course, Mom vehemently denied all of these needs. She fought this edict with all her might because their rent would nearly double, and, more pressing, a purge of her possessions would be necessary. They would have to move to a smaller apartment with two tiny closets.

Many angelic friends got me through this storm. The archangel was Jessa's mother-in-law, Joey. She offered her pickup truck and had much more patience with Mom than I ever had.

Together, she and I hauled many truckloads of clothes to a charity, along with bins of paper. Joey took many items to her home. They were "treasures" Mom thought were going to Jessa rather than to charity. Mom reacted by buying more clothes at the on-site thrift shop.

We culled stashes of glassware, kitchenware, doodads, and knickknacks, the scope of which was astonishing coming out of a one-bedroom apartment. Mom treated me as her enemy if I disagreed with her and as her savior when she needed my organizational skills to sort, not dispose of her possessions. My reality check was Joey, who encouraged me to follow through with the purging.

The head nurse was aware that neither of them could walk and both were on many meds.

"That car of theirs must be off this campus by the end of the weekend," he ordered me.

Only one family member desperately needed that used, dented car: Fern. When we delivered the car to Fern, she finally had the freedom she needed to obtain a job, as well as to rent her own place. She was a soaring bird of happiness.

Mom was starring in her own episode of *Hoarders*. We all know the script too well. And Mom had always been paranoid about theft. She told me that people were coming into her apartment to steal her keys, her cash, and her account numbers. Though this was all imagined by Mom, it was Dad who was diagnosed with acute dementia. It was time to become their financial and medical power of attorney, if they'd allow it.

We planned our first family vacation in more than a decade by renting a beach home. Fern was now stable enough to be with us, Jessa was freed from the baby years, and Ford was through chasing his financial independence. The challenge was clearing everyone's work schedules.

Just prior to our departure, the phone rang. Drew, the minister at my parents' retirement home, said, "Your mom was found in a stairwell with bruises. She says she was going to visit her husband."

After a moment, he added, "Her sodium levels are dangerously low. She was taken to the local trauma hospital, but she has no broken bones or injuries. It's time for them to move into our skilled nursing care wing."

Within the week, the hospital discharged Mom, back to her grateful husband. Mom was anxious with short-term memory loss, and Dad's treatment at the VA ended, as he was too frail to travel by van and sit in waiting rooms, even with kindly Dave, Joey's husband, escorting him. The on-site doctors of the skilled care unit would treat them both now.

Post vacation, I provided my signed power of attorney to my parents' doctors and banks. Mom had lived like a pauper when she had no need to. She hoarded her money as well. She had never been truthful with me *or* Dad about their total worth. I gently posed the question of why to her.

"It was none of your business!" she responded. "We want to make sure we have enough to move down to you and get an apartment and a caretaker!"

We had never heard of this plan before. Reality would soon be crashing down with their move into assisted living.

When we visited in the summer, we were surprised that it was Family Day. Had Mom invited us? No, but you can bet she invited Oh-So-Nice-Joey, as Ryan called Jack's mom, because Mom let me know Joey was perfect in every way and had married only once. Joey *was* an angel.

My parents were given one last chance by their care team to prove they could live in their apartment. By now, Mom loved the unit because we had worked so hard to reduce the piles of clutter, yet she was sneaking out to do laundry despite this prohibition. She found self-worth in doing laundry and ironing, as the mandatory imposed fifteen-dollar-per-week fee was, as she called it, "highway robbery."

Dad slept more than he was awake. His cognition was being affected by his hearing loss. Sadly, the hearing aids he received from the VA were substandard. I ordered the best on the market since learning they could certainly afford it, but Mom was furious with me for doing so. Her anger fueled my own anger, as Dad deserved the best, and I told her so. She forever held a grudge against me for this purchase, despite the fact that each morning when his nurses dutifully inserted them into his ear canals, Dad proclaimed, "I have not heard this clearly in many years! It is wonderful to hear everyone!"

I decided to take Mom's diamond rings, at the direction of the head nurse. He said they did not want valuable jewelry in assisted living. One ring had already been cut off when she fell, and her finger swelled as a result. When she later asked for the rings to be returned, I explained, "They were promised to your granddaughters, who will inherit my rings when I am your age."

"I want to sell them to use the money to hire a cabinet maker for my kitchen," she said. "I want to store my teacups, saucers, and trays, so I can properly serve tea for six."

"When you cannot walk, you cannot entertain, but why don't we go furniture shopping?"

I knew she had the funds, and I would do my part to help her feel at home in her new apartment.

Using the store-provided wheelchair, we found a small café table, sturdy Amish hardwood chairs, a bed and mattress, and a comfy leather recliner. She was elated until Dad kept falling out of his new bed. Thankfully the store came and took the bed back despite the gash from the scooter, but by law the mattress could not be returned. The maintenance crew had to lug a one-week-old premium mattress away to storage. I will always hope that some underpaid aide now sleeps better. It was not long before the recliner smelled of urine and the chairs and table were demolished by scooter ramming. But, I decided, if all the new furniture had made Mom temporarily happy, it was well worth the price.

When we visited in August, the windows were open, with the air-conditioner blasting.

"Dad likes to feel a breeze," Mom explained.

I looked for Dad then, and I found him on the bathroom floor.

When he first saw me standing above him, he said, "I spent the night here. Mom said not to bother the aides because I fell yesterday, and they came then to help." He did not even try to rebut the crazy logic of his wife.

"I slept on the floor once before when we moved, out of desperation," whined Mom, coming into the bathroom.

"You're no longer in desperation. People are paid here to help him up!" I was emphatic.

When an aide came a few moments later to help, Mom said, "This is my daughter, who's been married three times."

"Yes, Mom, everyone here knows this fact by now," I said before releasing my long, audible sigh.

***

Soon the facility informed me their fourth month in assisted living would be their last. A double room was available, awaiting them in the skilled nursing unit. Several reasons necessitated the move: their inability to walk without holding onto furniture, multiple falls, noncompliance with laundry, and messes found in their bathroom by their overworked aides.

Mom went on a tirade when I told her that until her apartment was empty, she would be double-billed. Then she had a total change of heart in accepting my help of working ten hours straight to organize, donate, trash, and prioritize her possessions yet again. Ryan came along on this trip to help me load our car with family photos, knickknacks, and Mom's antique accordion, all of which would not fit in my airplane luggage. We made the drive home over the mountains.

Dad continued falling in the assisted living wing. He could barely get out of his bed. Mom continued to fear running out of money, even with Ryan updating her monthly about the state of her finances.

In late fall, Mom was admitted to the hospital with sepsis and became unresponsive. Miraculously, she steadily improved in a week's time and was discharged just in time for Dad's last birthday party.

We celebrated Dad's ninety-third birthday in a private dining room with the whole family. We surprised him with Ford's arrival and two slide shows, one from his eightieth birthday and a new one Ford made from old slides called "The Early Years." Wine, flowers, and cake were nice additions, but the elders were most thrilled by their great-grandsons, who were well-behaved and respectful throughout the festivities.

***

Obesity-related congestive heart failure results in increased fluid retention necessitating increased medications and decreased mobility. Taping Mom's legs would have helped, but she removed the tape. She said it did not match her outfit or shoes. "It's bedlam here," was her new catch phrase, which she repeated whenever she saw us.

By midwinter Mom was hospitalized due to elevated sodium and lowered oxygen levels. This meant days of me traveling between her hospital room and Dad's nursing home room. He became anxious and frightened without his wife at his side. When he learned she would be discharged back to him, he was euphoric.

"You are wonderful," he told me, as if it were all my doing. He miraculously began eating, sleeping, and socializing better in response to her return.

We all knew Mom was herself again when she said staff had stolen from her. Unfortunately, this time it was true. Her wallet was found on the floor with eighty-nine dollars missing. The money was refunded to my parents' account by the main office. This incident rewarded and increased her paranoia.

One night she was determined to sneak over to her old laundry room, where she fell and was unable to get up for more than two hours. The result was a new bracelet that beeped when she left the unit, a needed gift in time for her ninety-first birthday party. Fern, Brian, Joey, and Dave joined us for her favorite Chinese takeout in a private room with flowers. A photo shows her holding her favorite yellow roses. She actually looked happy, a rarity.

On my next monthly visit, Mom looked pasty white and complained of stomach cramps. We stayed for two days, but by the time we arrived back home, she was in the hospital near death. She never told the hospital she had a daughter who was her medical power of attorney. Instead, she gave permission for her emergency bowel resection surgery at three in the morning while I slept, unaware. The doctor said she had a slim chance of recovery with the edema in her legs proving her decreased heart functioning, so of course I flew right back to Pittsburgh after receiving this call.

"She's been cut and has cancer!" Dad said when he first saw me in his room. I assured him this was not the case.

I spent my time traveling between the hospital, Dad's room, and the cozy guestrooms of my friends. Within four days, Mom made yet another miraculous recovery, but her surgeon looked right at her and said, "I wish I could say you will recover, but your heart will eventually do you in. You need to be on a heart-healthy diet, which could prolong your life." The truth didn't hurt, nor did it help, unfortunately.

He left us. She looked at me. "I'm not much bigger than you. Our wrists are the same."

It took three aides to transfer her from bed to chair to toilet, with the help of a Hoyer lift.

On the advice of our personal banker, we met with her ex-sister-in-law, an estate attorney resembling Tammy Faye Bakker. She gave us this advice, matching her colorful appearance, "Take ten thousand dollars a day out of the account at a branch office near you. Put it in a safety deposit box. And *that* is precisely how you will get out of paying the taxman!"

That was our last meeting, as we did not want to end up in jail for tax evasion.

An attorney at our church stressed gifting to family members, which was perfectly legal for a power of attorney. When I made the suggestion that Mom could gift her great-grandkids and grandkids rather than pay a large death tax to the state, Mom asked, "You mean fourteen thousand to each?" Then she waved me off. "That's preposterous."

She changed the subject quickly. But I initiated the gift transactions anyway, as was my legal right to do so. I understood the tax ramifications and put smiles on my children's faces.

At the next care team meeting, the issue was weight. Dad needed to gain some, and Mom needed to lose some. Mom said she hated living there, so the doctor recommended weight goals be proposed as incentives to move out of skilled nursing. But Mom snuck out every night to the snack cart in the dining room and could not be redirected. The nurses explained that these high-calorie snacks were for patients with loss of appetite.

"I get lonely. Dad sleeps all the time, so I eat."

A month later she had gained eight pounds.

Dad lost eight pounds and wore size thirty-six pants. We purged the room of seventeen size forty-two pants because Mom could not toss any of Dad's clothes out.

"He might need them, if…when…," she would say.

It takes an angel to be a compassionate certified nurse's aide for years on end. Diane was that angel for my folks. She told me that she was to be taken off of my parents' care because of a new supervisor's rotational system. I told that supervisor I would pull my parents out pronto unless Diane stayed with them. My advocacy paid off, and Diane remained on their care team.

***

Dad loved it when I would push him outside in his wheelchair to the gazebo in the garden. Mom led the way on her electric scooter. Once there, they immediately fell asleep. I learned to bring a book to read.

I clearly remember Dad waking and saying to his wife, "I love you, Marie. I give you all the credit for my success in life." Then he nodded off.

"You call this a marriage?" Mom asked me, once he fell into a steady snore again.

"Yes, I do," I said calmly, though furious with her. Most of the other female residents were widows.

***

The best plans were laid for their last wedding anniversary party. Those plans went awry. Dad woke up too ill to attend church with his family. So, while Fern and Brian went to church with Mom, Dad was taken by ambulance to the ER with a possible stroke, unable to speak. He had had a brain seizure caused by a new anti-depressant prescribed *without* my consent.

Neurological reactions occur with frail folks in their nineties. The head facility physician never apologized. Though I see myself as an effective advocate, I am not fond of litigation. And I pick my battles.

As a result, Dad permanently lost his beloved VA-provided scooter because he was too weak to transfer. In fact, it was time for hospice services. His ability to reason was affecting his actions. For example, in the skilled nursing dining room, he once quietly reached for a glass, urinated in it under the tablecloth, then returned it to the drink cart. It could have easily been mistaken for apple juice by another resident. On another occasion, he awakened in the night and rifled through drawers, disturbing Mom's sleep, without a clue what he was looking for.

***

"When can I get Dad's scooter? It's better than mine," Mom asked.

"Mom, that's not my concern," I told her.

"Well, what should be your concern?" she asked, as if *my* priorities were all wrong.

"Well, have you given any thought to drafting your own obituaries?" I asked.

She shook her head no and looked at me as though I were from some faraway planet.

"Well, Mom, that will be on *my* to-do list after my ninetieth birthday."

"Why don't you and Ryan work on Dad's obituary and I will approve it," she ordered.

It did not occur to her that we should draft up one for her, too, but we did.

Dad existed on ice cream bars. I walked to the main kitchen and informed the chef of this. He kindly handed me all the Klondikes from his freezer and told me to return whenever Dad asked. The hospice nurse taught us that the last food an elderly person wants is often a sweet milk product.

Hospice provided Dad with a reclining, padded, high-end wheelchair, a true godsend. Once he was less likely to fall out of his chair, Dad was more comfortable and had more freedom to maneuver himself about. At times Dad was totally aware, especially when he video-chatted with Jessa and her boys. He was elated to see his great-grandsons on a live-action screen.

"I'll be one hundred on my next birthday, but I'm afraid I'll be leaving you soon," he told me after this call. "I know I am going to be in Heaven, but I hate to leave you."

"Dad, you'll be ninety-three. I'll be just fine, no worries," I assured him, tears in my eyes.

He became more appreciative, while Mom became morose and was finally prescribed an anti-depressant. She asked me to send her cash for an upcoming craft fair. When I forgot, she was "so very disappointed" in me. The wing manager saved me with a loan; I repaid her with cash and a pampering gift on my next visit. During that same visit, I walked into the kitchen one day to get more Klondike bars, and I found Mom alone in the café eating a doughnut, unaware that she had been seen.

When she returned, Dad said to her, "Thank you for standing by me all these years and taking care of me."

She practically turned on her heels right then to leave again. "I am going to dinner in the dining room, as I just have got to get out," she responded. Her weight continued to be an issue.

The biggest challenge in my life was making sure my mother did not go completely crazy…and take me with her.

CHAPTER TWENTY-NINE
Dead Ball

Ryan and I moved to our retirement home on the lake, with an expansive fishing dock, a deck with a fire table, and huge windows in the open living area, perfect for watching sunsets. This was what we'd saved and scrimped for our whole lives. It was a long way from tenement housing in New Jersey for me or base housing for Ryan. We did not tell my parents until we had been settled in for a month. Dad was excited to see photos proving that I could happily go fishing to my heart's content anytime, just a few steps from our back door.

An early memory I have from my childhood is my first trip to Lake Warren with Dad. My tangerine children's fishing pole is still in use by my grandsons. Sixty years ago, I first baited a fat worm and cast its line into waters teaming with hungry "sunnies" and "catties." Dad was so proud the day he told Mom that under his tutelage, I had out-caught him at age five. In recurring dreams, I am fishing with my Dad, and to this day, catching a fighting catfish thrills me, always taking me back to those long-ago sparkling waters by his side. It's no wonder my photos of my private fishing pier pleased him.

***

I planned what I was sure was Dad's last birthday party, his ninety-third. Ten guests in the main dining room would include Ford's new girlfriend, Tanya. Though she'd renounced her Mormon faith, Mom called her "the little Mormon girl." The entire family liked this new girlfriend.

Dad was alert and appropriate throughout his party and enjoyed the gifts, but more, he relished all the attention from family members when he sat at the head of the table and blew out his candles. This party was mere weeks before Christmas.

Fern was in charge should any crisis with her grandparents arise over the holidays while we went on a Disney Christmas cruise with Jessa and her family. It was a miracle that she was now in a responsible familial position. Thankfully, all was calm and bright in Pittsburgh while we were away. From the moment they boarded the grand ship, our grandsons thoroughly believed in the Disney magic around them.

We told the boys that this cruise would be their only big Christmas gift from us. At age three, Cole believed this new lifestyle of the rich and famous would be his forever. When he realized he would have to disembark from the ship, he had a tantrum, screaming to his parents, "This is my Christmas gift from Gammylee and Grampa! I like my new bedroom and my new school here. I don't want to go back to my old ones!"

Wouldn't we all like to imagine our most wonderful vacations lasting forever? And Gray's cruise highlight was shooting down the water slides with me enough times to make this grandma dizzy.

***

On our next visit to see my parents, Mom came out with this pearl of wisdom: "You know your father's heart condition was caused by the saccharin he had in the war."

"Mom, the pink packets are used daily by millions. They do not cause heart conditions," I told her.

She looked at me as though I were just plain stupid.

Dad was on Zoloft and asked me, "Are we behind enemy lines? Is NATO in charge? When do you think we will get out?"

"Just where is it that you want to go, Dad?" I asked him gently.

"I just want the whole family to be together." He looked at me with a sweet smile.

Dad had been on 100-percent military disability for years because of PTSD, although we never saw him as disabled. He was saner and healthier than Mom had been their whole lives.

At Mom's next care team meeting, the nurses said she was getting out for art club and Scrabble often. This socialization put her in a better state of mind. She asked us to buy her wine for her Monday night girlfriend parties. We happily obliged and bought her two Riesling bottles. After Ryan reviewed her finances, Mom confessed that she was very worried about her money running out.

"Ryan has done the math. You will run out at age one hundred and ten," I soothed her.

"I want to travel," she countered. "I want to go to Philadelphia and see my old neighborhood. I want to go to Germany and stay for a month." Her reality was crumbling around her like a sugar cookie.

We visited her in March on her ninety-second birthday, with balloons and gifts in hand.

As soon as we arrived, she told me to look for Dad's hearing aids. When opening a night table drawer, I found it full of hundreds of every kind of condiment, enough to supply a snack bar. Besides salt, pepper, teabags, ketchup, and jellies, she stashed butter and creamers.

"They took away my vacuum cleaner and my iron, so I had to have them," she muttered.

The next day we visited our old church on Palm Sunday. It was a welcome break from hours in the nursing home, hearing the large choir we once sang with and seeing familiar faces.

"I need a knife to field dress the deer you shot," Dad said when we got to their residence.

"Dad I never shot a deer, but Ryan caught and ate a rattlesnake in the Navy," I diverted.

Dad had no appetite, so we three had Chinese takeout with Mom in the atrium she loved.

"It is a very sad birthday because Dad is going to die soon. Did you bring his obituary?" Mom asked. She approved of it but never asked to see the one we had written for her.

Three days after our visit, Mom's nurse called and said she was not doing well.

"I am so tired. They tell me my oxygen and salt levels are off," Mom said on the phone.

"Then you should go to the hospital. If you are not better tomorrow, I will be flying in."

"I love you," she said, and after all of her negativity, I knew she did, as best she was able.

By late evening she was unresponsive in ICU, and her bloodwork revealed a heart attack.

The day before Easter, there were no plane seats until afternoon. A doctor called and said she was fading. Their minister, Drew, went to Mom's side and prayed, as did Jack's mother, Joey.

Just before our airport departure, the ICU nurse called to say Mom had died peacefully with no pain, just one shallow last breath while sleeping. Joey confirmed her death was easy.

When we arrived at the retirement community, we met with Pastor Drew to plan Mom's service and then walked to Dad's room to find him alert.

With Ryan, Drew, and the hospice nurse, I summoned enough strength to tell him, "Dad, Mom went to Heaven yesterday."

We all saw the shock and pain shoot across his face.

"Can I have some time now alone with my wife?" he asked after we prayed in a circle.

We left, and Ryan watched from the hall as Dad went into an almost spiritual trance talking to Mom's spirit, then fell into a deep sleep. I stayed in his room while Ryan ran errands.

"I never thought she'd go first. I so badly want to go with her," he said upon awakening.

"You will when it is time," I said.

His quiet acceptance of this fact was admirable.

My mother had been busy feeling sorry for herself over her husband's impending death. She had never prepared for her own. She never got the chance to say her goodbyes to Dad and me.

Looking back, it makes sense that she was taken prior to him because he was always the stronger one. He handled her loss and his own coming death far better than his wife would have handled his. He was also easier to care for in every way possible, throughout his demise.

The next morning, Diane got Dad ready to go to Easter church service with us. He was alert when Drew announced Mom's passing. Afterward, he received the sympathy of his friends.

Then we began the *final* downsizing of Mom's possessions in the room while Dad slept.

***

Eight days later, with April snowflakes falling, we picked up Mom's ashes and devoted one last, final, full day to extensive purging. We cleared out one side of the room to avoid a bill of more than three hundred dollars per day. Dad sincerely thanked us both for finishing the job.

A few weeks later we met the entire family at the perfectly manicured National Cemetery of the Alleghenies on a lovely spring morning. After Drew's concise, personal eulogy, we drove directly to see Dad, who was far too frail to attend the outdoor service.

I wheeled Dad to the front of a full chapel for Mom's memorial service.

Dad sang along with all of the chosen hymns, even to the chorus of "Danny Boy" with the soloist. Ford gave a touching family eulogy about his "Gigi," never faltering or reading notes. After Drew spoke of her many gifts of time to her retirement community, he offered the microphone to the audience. Dad extended a trembling hand toward the microphone.

"I could not have chosen a better wife and mother to my daughter. I loved her," he said.

There wasn't a dry eye in the chapel, and Dad greeted all with love and dignity afterward.

The next day Dad sat in the atrium with his granddaughters, coherently conversing, and I asked him, "Have you ever thought of moving south, Dad?" The family witnessed his answers.

"I am open to moving down south if that is easier for you," he said. *Duh. One down.*

"Dad do you know what an advocate is?" I asked, recalling my career as an advocate.

"Of course, I do. That's a person who acts on behalf of another." He was all there then.

"I am your advocate now, and you must make an important decision. Do you want to stay here where you know and love everyone, but are far from me, or do you want to move south where you will not know anyone, but you will see me every day?" I carefully asked.

"Oh, I want to be near you. Besides, I can always make new friends," he said emphatically.

"Do you want to travel in a van all day or in a private plane for one hour?" I asked.

"I want a plane ride!" he said with a smile. I immediately gave notice he'd be moving.

***

After this conversation, my dear old friend, Liz, whom I had not seen in years, visited him. I had called her to tell her Dad had asked about her, remembering our life-long friendship.

When Liz came into Dad's room, we hugged for many minutes. The years and the distances that had passed between us were too vast to count. Her voice was coarse and gravely from years of nicotine abuse. But her beauty and sense of humor were still her greatest gifts.

"You're still a handsome man, know that?" she said coyly to Dad, underestimating him.

"Liz, you're full of shit, you know that?" he said as we belly-laughed along with him.

Dad was doing far better than expected. Maybe he *could* make the big move south without it killing him.

CHAPTER THIRTY
Hall of Very Good

We worked quickly over a month's time to make the move happen: transportation, medical records, moving his belongings in large suitcases via our trips on Ryan's airline, and lastly, arranging his new placement. Dad would live in a facility six miles from our home, nicer in every way, for far less rent! This was the same place Mom had balked at over a scooter deposit. I was in charge now, and I was proceeding with the move my father wanted and deserved.

On Memorial Day, we visited Mom's grave, surrounded by flags honoring service members. I know she would feel, as I will someday, that it is truly an honor to be buried as a spouse amidst so many souls who served our country.

We packed up the last of Dad's belongings in three small suitcases. On moving day, Dad told me he was glad to be leaving the facility, despite many tears from the staff as we departed. A Cheyenne turboprop awaited us at the corporate terminal. There was no TSA or x-ray machines, and we didn't have to provide identification cards. Private airplane transportation was quite a different ballgame. An airport valet brought us coffee during our short wait with our van driver.

He drove us right up to the plane where Dad was hoisted through a door via a bed sheet and a strong EMT. Ryan sat in the copilot seat. I sat facing my father in the rear of the cramped cabin.

A paramedic took Dad's vitals during the bumpy ride through the clouds…and he loved the ride. Once we landed, he was eased into our car for the short drive to his new residence. His name was already on the doorplate of room 514.

After we unpacked his belongings, he met staff and two veterans, and we left him playing bingo with them. When we returned later in the day, an aide had taken him on a tour. She said he had casually mentioned to her that she had really big boobs, after which he went to his new bed exhausted and slept peacefully.

"I would love to think we could have just three more months with him here," I told Ryan, at the end of that long moving-in day. I hoped to have quality time with him before he died and I chose this arbitrary time period, a stretch far longer than the hospice team would estimate.

Hospice quickly accepted Dad because he was wasting away, termed "failure to thrive." Daily, I treated him to either an extra thick milkshake or a smoothie to supplement his diet. I hired a beautiful geriatric massage therapist. She visited weekly and adored him.

"No funny stuff! Hear that down there?" he said when they first met, ever the jokester.

One day, he said to me, "Can I ask you a question? Why is it taking me so long to die?"

"Because God is in charge," I replied, after thinking for a moment. "Maybe, this time is a gift to me. I'm not ready to say goodbye."

He gave me a smile that I felt flow warmly from my eyes down to my heart, as he told me he loved me.

An aide heard Dad was Irish and took us both into the room of an Irish war bride. Dad sang "Danny Boy" in his sweet tenor voice of ninety-three years, and the old lass was enraptured.

Two weeks after the move, we decided to drive him to our new home for a visit. It was not easy transporting him in and out of our car, into the wheelchair and up steps, but we did it. He beamed when we took him up to each window that looks out onto the shimmering lake, and said, "What an upgrade from your last house. A real bargain! I bet you paid twenty thou more for this."

Then in the car, Dad said, "That was a lovely parting gift, to take me to see your home."

We were touched by his understanding, for that is precisely what it had been.

On days like this, he was all there cognitively. Other days he was frustrated, searching for his keys and his wife. His bloodwork showed nothing alarming. He simply did not want to eat. On Father's Day, we took him a card with his milkshake, and I asked him this question, "Dad, you have more money than you need. What would you think about gifting each of your grandkids what the government allows to be tax-free, from you?"

"You do whatever you think is right. I trust you totally."

What a difference from Mom.

Dad came alive when a fabulous entertainer sang for an hour in the nursing wing. Music still invigorated him. He danced in his wheelchair and, when that man suddenly held up the microphone in front of his withered face, he harmonized perfectly to "You Are My Sunshine."

My best friends met Dad. Greg told him of my next role in a play he'd written. As he left, Dad told him to take care of me. He met two of my W-2 choir friends and my favorite newest neighbor, Angie. He was charming to all, glad to know I'd actually made friends in the South.

Then Jessa and her family visited him. He called each by name as he said he loved them. He played corn hole with his great-grandsons and saw photos of their first fish, caught from our dock.

***

Looking back, it is clear that a beautiful transformation came about when Dad moved nearer to me. In the North, most of his staff were Caucasian. In the South, Dad was cared for by a dark-skinned angelic aide named Mary. She met him with a loving smile and warm hug each time she entered his room. A similar beauteous angel named Janice kept his room spotless. Janice worked with an open Bible placed atop her cleaning cart. When she prayed for a person, it was palpable. One of his best nurses was gorgeous LaTonya. These women fell for my father, and he in turn fell hard for them. He had morphed into a man without prejudice, opening his arms to these women's all-consuming love and care. He was finally able to see through to people's hearts, regardless of their color. It was his spiritual gift to me, the most priceless by far.

***

By the time Fern visited in July, Dad was unresponsive, sleeping, drooling, and quiet. The next day, Ryan's sister came to visit. He was once again unresponsive, even while listening to a music program. Why? The staff observed apnea and gave him Morphine, *only* to be administered for pain. He told me he did not *want* morphine and was not *in* any pain. As the drug abated, he became more lucid, though the hospice nurse said he had only hours to live. We said our goodbyes and went to eat a quick dinner. When we returned, Dad met us in his wheelchair, arms raised up at seeing his granddaughter, and said, "Get me out of here. I'm hungry, Fern!" Fern giddily fed him pudding and ice cream.

He was joyous at seeing her and told her he loved her while purposely speaking in fluent German, remembering that all of his grandchildren studied the language in high school.

Fern's trip had been extended because no airplane seats were available. She actually was grateful for this. She saw Dad at his best. He rallied one last time for the grandkid he had so missed for more than a decade.

Ryan's son, Adam, came to visit. Dad recognized him and said he had heard much about him over the years. Adam was finally free from addiction's grip. He was doing well as an electrical inspector for a large city, was seeing his twin sons monthly, and had a lovely, steady girlfriend with a professional career. Adam had truly turned his life around. It was a celebrated visit for all.

Dad's rally lasted two days, until he fell out of his wheelchair and sustained a concussion. He was bruised, cut, disoriented, and anxious.

He refused to eat and kept calling out randomly, "Momma" and "Oh, please."

I tried to get a high-end wheelchair rental like he had at his previous placement in Pittsburgh, but the home's administrator said *this* state's regulations considered them to be restraints. I appealed to an elder attorney and an ombudsman for the elderly. No one would help me. Inevitably he fell out of his bed and suffered a second concussion. I did not have the time or the energy to fight an idiotic state rule by myself.

He slept more, moaned more, and ate even less. It was hard to get through to him.

"Do you want to be with Mom in Heaven?" I asked him. When he answered yes, I said, "Just tell God you're ready, Dad. Ryan will take good care of me for the rest of my life."

"Eating won't get me any closer to Heaven," he told his nurse. And so, he didn't eat.

After his fall out of bed, his arm was purple with bruises. He was mostly unresponsive. His pupils grew small, his eyes glazed over, and he refused his milkshake. He became restless, tossing with terminal agitation, trying to get out of his bed. I called hospice to let them know the situation was worsening. It took both Ryan and me to keep Dad from ripping off his disposable brief and getting out of bed. We held the covers over him tightly for two hours before the hospice nurse arrived. She said though he was now on morphine, he needed anti-psychotic meds to calm him and ease his dying. Reaching out into thin air, he repeatedly said, "I want water," which he could not keep down. This was neither easy nor peaceful to witness. He did not have the luxury of the easy death I had prayed for, slipping away peacefully, as his wife did. My chest ached for him, and time slowed painfully.

On the day Fern turned thirty-three, I was sixty-three, and Dad was ninety-three. I did not want him to die on this day, which held joyful memories. The hospice team said he required constant sedation to calm his agitation.

Ryan went to see Dad alone. He told him, "I love your daughter. I will take care of her."

After that exchange, Dad slept more soundly, needing fewer drugs. Between singing hymns, I said, "Go to the light with your Marie." I went to church and prayed at the altar. We visited him in the late afternoon, sang more hymns and said our final goodbyes.

The morning of August twenty-sixth, *exactly* three months after he was moved south, he gently died in the early morning with no signs of distress and no medications. I was able to visit him daily for those three months. Now he is visiting with Mom in a sweeter place. They are singing, kissing, and laughing, young again in body and mind. That morning, Ryan and I awoke pre-dawn. We sat on our back deck, drinking coffee, and watched a perfectly full moon setting on the lake's silvery horizon. Two monarch butterflies flitted around and between us.

Ford visited us two weeks later, when he had intended to see his "Pop" for the last time. We flew together to Pittsburgh, where we met Jessa. We four arrived at the National Cemetery, where Fern and Brian awaited. Despite the light, misty rain, almost fifty people came to honor Dad. Many were older vets involved in organizations with Dad. Three Air Force airmen presented military honors with a somber flag folding. Drew spoke briefly and eloquently of my father's unforgettable character, and then, at my request, Ford spoke even more eloquently of what his grandfather's legacy meant to him personally. Dad's American Legion Post solemnly presented me with a Bible. I requested that Ford be presented with the flag that draped the ashes. Dad had been so proud of his grandson, the son he and Mom never had. Pop had been the most steady and stalwart male *throughout* Ford's life. Ryan stood tall and supportive in the back of the shelter, after nobly and quietly giving his seat to a frail elderly lady.

Drew recited The Lord's Prayer and the Twenty-Third Psalm. A uniformed Air Force bugler played "Taps." It was the tribute Dad had wanted and deserved. He was with us in spirit.

The five of us walked to Mom's newly chiseled headstone. Pop's ashes were to be buried next to his wife, imminently. We celebrated Dad with an Irish wake in a Chinese restaurant steps away from my old office space where Ryan and I first set eyes on each other. A toast was made by Ryan to my parents. Then all went their way. Ryan and I were left on our own when I posed this question: "Do you think when your parents die, they can exert any influence on their loved ones back here?"

"I believe going to Heaven for a spirit is like a baby coming out of a womb. There are no memories or cares of one's previous life here," my theologically well-versed husband answered.

"I believe our dearly departed have the ability to guide us toward wiser choices," I replied, "and if they have any power at all, they are going to get Fern out of that God-forsaken city that she's been stuck in. Mom and Dad knew that was my prayer for over a decade now. Let's just see how long it takes."

I confided this thought only to Ryan.

CHAPTER THIRTY-ONE

Grand Slam

It took less than six months for the spirits of my ancestors to have their Heavenly powwow. In the new year, Brian sadly traded the illegal drug addiction, which he had overcome, for an addiction to hard liquor. Fern did not like being around an emotionally abusive drunk any more than I did with her father years ago. Brian came home drunk every day and drank until he blacked out. After he ignored her ultimatum, Fern left him at the end of summer, moving a long day's journey away, to a new sales career, with new friends, where she feels relieved and at peace.

Thanks, Mom, Dad, Nana, and Aunt Peg for the powwow. I will have so many questions and much gratitude for you all at our next reunion.

***

My very first fortune in my Great Aunt Marjorie's birthday book was prophetic, predicting my life to be graced with talent in the arts and traveling the world. I have been given the opportunity to travel to places I never knew existed from Scandinavia to the South Pacific, Edmonton to Ecuador, and many exotic places in between. I have been able to luxuriate in the arts that bring me such joy by singing, writing, painting, and acting. I cherish my chosen loyal friends who support me, as I do for them in return.

And my best friend is my caring, strong husband who blesses my life abundantly. At last, my first character onstage has been actualized. Wendy has found her adult Peter Pan, who keeps her young in thought and flies her to magical places around the world while we still can. My guardian angel pushed me to get out that phone book and start calling down the columns of numbers. For me, the third time at bat was the grand slam. My three children were on the loaded bases, in the same tough game, and with Ryan's help, and God's help, we all made it safely back to our home base.

CHAPTER THIRTY-TWO
Post-Game Wrap-Up

As I reflected upon my six-plus decades of memories once my parents were laid to rest, I felt the need more than ever to tell my story. My parents died within five short months of one another. Just as they instilled the faith of my ancestors in me as a child, I saw to it that they were laid to rest with the power of Christ present. The evil of addiction has reared its ugly head too many times in my life. If I did not have faith in a higher power, I would be a weak, lonely, miserable woman. I pray daily for His strength, guidance, forgiveness, and wisdom. He is my personal God who gives me peace when the world around me is in a state of craziness, which is often. Long ago I learned to pray specifically for my needs and to work hard myself toward my goals, which often change in unexpected ways. With wisdom comes power and direction. I believe that angels *do* guide and protect us and our loved ones.

Having faith and praying, however, sure did not stop me from making mistakes in my life. I rushed into relationships too fast and for the wrong reasons. I didn't get to really know the families I was marrying into. Maybe one should thoroughly check the health of the tree's roots, trunk, and branches before committing to nest in it. Your children will reflect you both, good and bad, like it or not. Addictions, mental illness, learning disabilities, and personality traits all pass down through family trees. In no time at all the children will want to leave your nest in the tree and feather their own. As they go where their careers and families dictate, they may not fly back often. Fly to their nest, then, but do not overstay.

My story is told from the perspective of being an only child because it is all I know. I surely did not want this for my own children. Only-child status becomes hardest when your parents become feeble and illogical. Most old folks do not mellow into sweet, soft marshmallows. Some turn into stale licorice. Siblings may be jealous of you or try to rival you, but you can bounce ideas and decisions concerning your parents' end off of them because they share the same history. Death places big responsibilities on an only child. When your folks die, you are the only person in the world to keep their life-long memories. Your children will only remember them as older people.

I try with all my might not to be judgmental of others. Lord knows Mom judged me on my three marriages. My third time at bat, I hit a grand slam. I have seen many women shrivel up like bitter prunes after divorce. As Liz advised me, cry for three days and say, "Excess baggage." There are good men in the world, but you have to open your heart and prayers to at least one. And it is never too late to find love.

But I did finally do something right. I made my spouse my best friend. At times he can annoy me more than all my friends combined, but he is my first and last confidant, sexual experiment, and travel partner. A sharp intellect and a kind heart mean much more than movie-star looks and toned bodies. Here's a reality: We all sag and bag eventually. How lovely to be held in those trusted, familiar, and likewise saggy arms at one's end. The loving touch and adoring words of a committed spouse give comfort, no matter one's age or condition. And speaking of one's condition, there's something to be said about your body being a temple. If you fill yourself with poison, you will look and feel older earlier. Tobacco, booze, drugs, sugar, unhealthy fats, and unprotected exposure to the sun are your enemies.

Full-bodied red wine, dark chocolate, fresh seafood, and sunscreen are your friends, or at least they are mine, in moderation. Tasty treats give comfort, no matter one's age or condition. But treats are treats by definition, only if they are occasionally given.

I am blessed that Ryan allowed me to pursue my passion in the arts. You will know you have found your passion when time zips by while you are pursuing it. Try to leave behind some form of creativity and/or original thought by the time you meet your end. If nothing else, journal to preserve your memories, and be your own cheerleader. Record your kindnesses that help others soar. Give loved ones deserved compliments and encouragement. They might not get it elsewhere. We can love one another easily through our kind words, followed by our kind deeds.

Once I heard a minister preach a whole sermon on sex. Here's what I got out of it: Don't withhold or try to control sex. Give gladly. If you withhold it, others just might provide. A God-given gift, it circulates your blood, gives you needed exercise, and provides, hopefully, deep, revitalizing breaths.

Give it outside of marriage, and you will lose all logic and set yourself up for hurt and scorn. End of sermon.

Nana Marie told me, "What does not kill you makes you stronger." I am one strong woman. When you have a baby die, go through two failed marriages to alcoholics, and survive your own children's struggles with addiction, you grow into a sturdy oak tree. We all have our unique crosses to bear. Each crisis brings hard lessons with it. And eventually, opportunities make themselves known to us like softly glowing, beckoning doors in a pitch-black room.

Be brave enough to open the doors by yourself. Know that you can do whatever you set your mind, heart, and spirit to accomplish. Take it from this little, old, ordinary grandma, one who has been around the bases a few times.

Acknowledgments

Thanks to my publishers Mindy and Amy for taking a chance on this very personal book.

Thanks to my editors Beth, Karli, and Monika for their skill and patience in making me actually sound like an author.

Thanks to my many sister-friends for reading my raw script, giving me the confidence to keep writing.

Thanks to my dear brother-friend Greg for being my creative muse in all of the arts.

Thanks to my incredibly strong and supportive children, Jessa, Fern, and Ford, for going to bat with me and still loving me, but not as much as I do you.

Thanks to my husband, Ryan, for being my third and final time at bat and for making every precious day with you a day to be grateful for.

www.ingramcontent.com/pod-product-compliance
Lightning Source LLC
LaVergne TN
LVHW041331080426
835512LV00006B/400